ICT for Teaching Assistants

The role of ICT in enhancing both teaching and learning in classrooms continues to develop, no more so than when in the hands of effective practitioners. This easy-to-use book outlines the many ways in which ICT can be used, both as a subject and as a tool to support learning across the curriculum.

Now fully updated to take into account innovations in ICT and the revised National Occupational Standards, *ICT for Teaching Assistants* looks at the impact of these changes and includes:

- practical examples of how ICT can be used, including web-based tools such as 'blogs' and 'wikis';
- guidance on working competently and safely on the internet;
- suggestions for activities with ideas for how these can be used in a variety of contexts;
- advice on gathering evidence to help build assessment plans;
- information on health and safety and legal requirements.

With links throughout to the National Occupational Standards for Teaching Assistants at Levels 2 and 3, this accessible book is essential for teaching assistants who wish to develop their confidence in ICT.

John Galloway is Advisory Teacher for ICT/SEN and Inclusion in the London Borough of Tower Hamlets. He also works as a consultant, trainer and freelance writer.

Hilary Norton is Advisory Teacher for ICT/SEN and Inclusion in the London Borough of Tower Hamlets. She also has a broad background in ICT in education, working as an ICT Coordinator in a mainstream primary school. She has worked in special schools for pupils with severe learning difficulties, profound and multiple learning difficulties, and social, emotional and behavioural difficulties. She also works as a consultant and trainer.

May 11 2021 23:26 PM
5/11/2021 1:14:58 PM

Katy Coysh

53 THORPE ROAD

NORWICH   NR1 1UD

UK

VAT: 939775170

Return Address: Unit 10 Castle Industrial CentreQueensferry Road UK, KY11 8NT

D3   Single - STA

UK1 Intexion   UK1-12-14-C1

KO-968-950   9781408868805   Used - Good

First Day at Bug School

Lloyd, Sam

AmazonUK   76072035

ICT for Teaching Assistants

Second edition

John Galloway

and

Hilary Norton

Routledge
Taylor & Francis Group

LONDON AND NEW YORK

First edition published 2004
by David Fulton Publishers

This second edition published 2011
by Routledge
2 Park Square, Milton Park, Abingdon, Oxon OX14 4RN

Simultaneously published in the USA and Canada
by Routledge
711 Third Avenue, New York, NY 10017

Routledge is an imprint of the Taylor & Francis Group, an informa business

British Library Cataloguing in Publication Data
A catalogue record for this book is available from the British Library

Library of Congress Cataloging-in-Publication Data
Galloway, John.
  ICT for teaching assistants/John Galloway, Hilary Norton. – 2nd ed.
  1. Education – Great Britain – Data processing.   2. Information technology –
  Great Britain.   3. Teachers' assistants – Great Britain.   I. Norton, Hilary.
  II. Title.
  LB1028.43.G348 2011
  371.33'4 – dc22   2010049140

ISBN13: 978–0–415–58306–0 (hbk)
ISBN13: 978–0–415–58307–7 (pbk)
ISBN13: 978–0–203–81585–4 (ebk)

Typeset in Bembo by
Florence Production Ltd, Stoodleigh, Devon

Printed and bound in Great Britain by
TJ International Ltd, Padstow, Cornwall

Contents

Introduction

The last few years have seen an increase in the number of adults in classrooms and the range of functions they perform. As these roles have developed so has the expectation that they will be filled by qualified staff. This has seen an expansion of the vocational qualifications framework for staff in schools, in particular for qualified teaching assistants.

These changes have seen support staff undertake tasks that had previously been part of the teacher's role. Many teaching assistants are now involved in the planning, delivery and assessment of education alongside the class teacher. They also teach small groups and individuals and supervise cover lessons. Many have developed expertise in particular areas, such as information and communication technology (ICT) or particular aspects of special educational needs (SEN).

This book will help support staff in classrooms understand how ICT is used for learning within the curriculum, combining background information with practical examples. There are illustrations throughout, and many explanations of how to perform particular tasks. When a specific action or function is mentioned it is placed in bold. There are also references in square brackets that indicate the particular aspects of the National Vocational Qualification (NVQ) for teaching assistants that are being referred to.

The NVQ for teaching assistants

The NVQ, whether in England or Scotland, is based directly on the National Occupational Standards for Supporting Teaching and Learning (STL) in Schools. There are sixty-nine of these standards listed on the Training and Development Agency for Schools (TDA) website, each identified as STL plus a number that designates its focus. The range of elements on offer recognises the diverse roles of support staff in schools, and should provide teaching assistants the opportunity to have their skills recognised with an accredited qualification regardless of the job they do. Level 2 has four mandatory units and three optional ones, while Level 3 has four mandatory units and six optional.

This book concentrates on STL 7 – Support the use of information and communication technology for teaching and learning, and STL 8 – Use of information and communication technology to support pupils' learning. The first of these fits within the framework for NVQ Level 2, whereas the second can also be used for NVQ Level 3.

The advantage of the NVQ is that it is based on a range of evidence, dependent on an individual's position. Unlike more traditional qualifications, there is no course as such, nor specified examinations or coursework. The teaching assistant takes the main responsibility for moving the qualification on through the portfolio they compile, supported by their assessor and their school mentor. The involvement of the school in evaluation means their achievement is fully understood at work.

To complete an NVQ you would need to gather together a portfolio of evidence to demonstrate that you can meet the Performance criteria (designated with P), which is what you need to show you can do, and the Knowledge base (shown by a K), which is what you need to show you know. These have been referenced throughout this book in square brackets. For example, '[STL 7.2 P2]' refers to the second part of Unit 7 – Support the use of ICT resources for teaching and learning, Performance criteria 2 'Give clear guidance and instructions on the use of ICT resources by others'.

Each candidate has an assessor who will help to plan how they will be assessed and what evidence to gather for the portfolio. This might include attending courses, answering verbal or written questions, and keeping a record of work with pupils. The assessor will also want to observe you. Generally the performance indicators headed, 'You must show', will need to be observed. However, this can be through role play and simulation. Within the unit, one piece of evidence can cover a number of criteria, and any piece of evidence can be used for more than one unit. There is a sample assessment plan shown as Appendix 2.

1

How we learn and how computers help

Those of us involved in education are all the time thinking about what our pupils need to learn and what is the best way that this can be achieved. Some of them will bury themselves in books for long periods, while others find it hard just to sit still, so we have to tailor what we do to help them to learn.

The introduction of computers into classrooms has brought about new tools for doing this, new ways of working and even new topics for study [STL 7 K1; STL 8 K2,3]. Working with computers is something all our pupils, regardless of skills and ability, need to know how to do, and quite often it is a way of working that leads to most (but not necessarily all) learners concentrating for longer periods of time than they would do otherwise, and helps them to become more creative while working with the powerful tools provided.

Computers also give quick and easy access to all sorts of knowledge. While it is still important to remember facts for instant recall, because of the introduction of technology into the classroom it is now possible quickly and easily to find much more information than our brains can hold, so rather than simply retaining knowledge we now need to know how to find it quickly and efficiently.

The web also allows us to be creators of information as well as consumers. The advent of blogs (online diaries), wikis (jointly created information sources), and video, music and photo sharing sites means that anyone anywhere in the world, regardless of their age, ability or location, can contribute to other people's knowledge and understanding of the world. Learning facts and figures is shifting towards learning about how to learn, how to find information and how to communicate and share it.

How human beings learn is the subject of constant research and debate, and our understanding of how the brain works is developing all the time, giving rise to new theories about how we gain, store and retrieve knowledge. We know that learning involves more than simply sitting quietly while someone at the front talks to us – and that people do not absorb everything they read or write down. In fact, people generally learn about:

10% of what they read,
20% of what they hear,
30% of what they see,
50% of what they both hear and see,
70% of what they say,
90% of what they simultaneously say and do.

(Ekwall, Shanker and James, *Diagnosis and Remediation of the Disabled Reader*, 3rd edition, 1988)

So to teach our pupils effectively we need to find a variety of different ways to get our message across. Simply reading a book is the least effective way of learning.

Computers are very powerful tools for changing how we work. They allow us to present material in different formats – as text, animation, sound, video or image – often simultaneously. A simple example is the use of subtitles on films, so we can hear what is being said and read it at the same time – useful for those who are studying a particular book, but also for people who are hearing impaired or learning another language.

Computers also provide the option of demonstrating what has been learned in different ways – not only can pupils write an answer, but they can also create an animation, record a song or annotate an image. Through the internet they can share their outputs with other pupils for comment and contrast, or to showcase their work, perhaps to relatives in distant places.

Developments in technology also mean a range of devices are available to use – not just computers such as desktops, laptops, notebooks and netbooks, but also pocket-sized devices, including mobile phones, MP3 players, iPods, iPhones and Blackberries, and games consoles such as the PSP or Nintendo DS. All of which are items you may find in your schools [STL 7 K2].

The internet provides the ability to access information in almost any place at almost any time and to create and share our own responses, reflection and reactions to where we are, what we are doing and what we see. Technology has revolutionised learning, and is continuing to do so.

Theories of learning

Debates about how people learn started long ago with the Ancient Greeks, and these debates continue today. Although staff in schools adopt very practical approaches in reaching their charges, they are often not too concerned with thinking about how learning is happening, as long as it works. Very few teachers consciously work with one particular theory or another (although in areas such as literacy, approaches are often structured around particular ideas – phonics in particular).

However, it is worth spending some time thinking about theories of learning as resources for computers, particularly software, are often created from a particular perspective about how children learn, and it may, or may not, suit what we are teaching. When choosing, or creating, software resources we need to be aware of the process of learning that it supports, as well as the content. This does not mean that you need to categorise everything as promoting a particular theory of learning, but rather that when using ICT you have given thought to how learning happens – in the NVQ there are several criteria where this is important [STL 7 K1,15; STL 8.1 P1,2,3,4 and K2,6,8,22,28].

There are two main theories about how we learn, Behaviourism and Constructivism. Both are in evidence in our classrooms today. Most teachers, probably without knowing it, will use different strategies that fall into each category.

In Behaviourist theory knowledge is seen as a change in behaviour, with our internal processes, such as thinking and remembering, being types of behaviour. Learning then becomes a process of imparting a body of knowledge to our pupils, and as the way they act, think and feel changes so learning is happening.

We can see this in primary schools today in the use of rote learning. Times tables are often learned by saying them out loud in unison. Children can learn that 'seven eights are fifty-six' even if they do not understand how the multiplication is worked out. Or another example is very young children repeating the alphabet even when they do not yet know which letter matches which sound. Or even that they are different sounds rather than one long string. As their behaviour changes – saying the different sounds and pointing to the corresponding letters for instance – so their understanding, that the two are linked, will also change, and they will then allocate the correct sound to each letter.

The second theory, Constructivism, is based on the idea that we all have our own, unique understanding of the world that we build as we learn new things. As we gain knowledge so we fit it in, relating it to what we already know and juggling ideas around so as to accommodate it. It is like a constantly changing jigsaw puzzle where we move the pieces around to fit each time we find a new bit so that we can make sense of the picture of the world we now have. This is the basis of discovery learning, where pupils are offered experiences from which they then extract their own learning. The role of the teacher is to provide challenges and new experiences for the children, and to guide them through these.

We could think of project work as Constructivist, where pupils follow their own course in learning, and teachers help them to make sense of what they find out, often raising questions that are a little harder than the children might ask if left to themselves.

Both theories have their supporters and their critics. Behaviourism is thought to be too restrictive, and Constructivism could mean pupils miss out on learning key knowledge. So what we tend to do in schools is to use a bit of both. Although children might chant times tables, they will also be colouring in number squares to spot the patterns the tables make. Sometimes we teach children the outcome and let the underpinning concepts follow, and sometimes we let them discover the concepts and point out particular outcomes later. In maths we might let pupils try out different ways of doing sums before showing them the standard notation.

Computers can be geared to either way of learning – they are tools that we adapt to our particular methods. Software can be seen as being developed from either perspective. Many revision programs, such as the BBC's Bitesize website, are based on multiple choice and can be seen as Behaviourist. If you get an answer wrong you can retry until you get it correct.

This way you can learn what is the correct answer to a question without necessarily understanding why it is right. This can be an effective way of working for remembering specific facts, but on its own it can lead to a rather boring educational diet.

The best known example of Constructivist approaches through ICT can be seen in 'Logo' style programs, such as 2Go and Softease Turtle from Softease. Here pupils can draw on screen using a 'turtle', an onscreen pointer, creating designs of increasing complexity, ranging from simple shapes to letters, numbers and patterns, all the time developing programs to tell the computer what to do. The process can be as simple as clicking on buttons to change direction, to writing a string of commands, each built up from other sub-programs. Teachers will provide the challenges – for instance, to write your own name – and show children how to write commands, but pupils will learn through trying things out rather than being directly told. All the time the teacher will ask questions and set new challenges.

Learning styles

We have five dominant senses, and unless one or more is severely impaired, we learn through all of them. In schools we generally work with sound and vision, reinforced with some tactile experiences, and barely acknowledging taste and smell, although these in themselves offer powerful prompts for our memory – you will probably have experienced the situation where a certain smell reminds you of a past event, such as your grandmother's perfume evoking thoughts of sitting on her knee being read to.

There have been many advances in recent years in our understanding of how the brain works and therefore how we learn. In schools there has been a lot of talk about learning styles, with the term VAK becoming widely used, referring to three dominant routes to learning – visual (seeing), aural (hearing) and kinaesthetic (moving or feeling). One instance where we can see these in action is in learning phonics. While repeating the sounds, and looking at the letter or phoneme on the interactive whiteboard, pupils often make an associated movement. For example, the 'ess' sound of the letter 'S' is associated with the fingers slithering along the forearm like a snake.

Computers can be a multisensory medium, combining sound and visuals in lively and stimulating ways that encourage learning. The more senses we can connect to, the more chance of reaching all of our pupils and helping them to learn.

Multiple intelligences

Howard Gardner suggests that there are eight intelligences:

- logical-mathematical – such as detecting patterns and reasoning things out
- linguistic – using language both orally and in writing, such as discussions or writing poems
- spatial – able to manipulate images mentally
- musical – can recognise elements of music and make up tunes

- bodily-kinaesthetic – able to coordinate one's own movements
- interpersonal – having an empathy for others, how they think and feel
- intrapersonal – being aware of our own thoughts and feelings
- naturalistic – awareness of one's environment.

This isn't to say that we can only learn in particular ways, simply that each of us have different strengths and we should look to exploit all of them in our teaching and learning. Each of us has these abilities to some degree; however, we all use some more successfully than others.

Computers allow us to work with all these different aspects of our pupils' intelligences. We can compose tunes, write, express our thoughts in many different ways, do complex sums and experiment with numbers. Many activities that previously required specialist skills and knowledge are now available to all of us. By using software we can produce the authentic sounds of any instrument and compose multilayered compositions without needing to be able to play a note or read music. We can do calculations in split seconds that used to take hours. We can try our hand at flying aeroplanes, and analyse in slow motion how we kick a ball. If we do not like the photo we have taken we can improve it to appear how we want it to look – perhaps making ourselves look thinner, or younger.

Whatever the activity, talking helps to reinforce learning. Ask your pupils to describe what they are doing, to talk through the steps of a task. Get them to explain to you, and to each other, how they have worked something out, or how they came to a particular answer. This is as valuable in ICT as in any other subject.

Summary

We have five senses, eight intelligences, two sides to the brain, two contrasting theories of learning and about a dozen subjects to teach. While it may seem difficult to juggle it all, ICT can be very helpful as it offers many possible ways to work. In some senses it can become an extension to our own brains, a place where we can find knowledge and be creative in hitherto impossible ways. In constructing our own understanding we can put these machines to use in a way no other tool allows.

All of us learn differently. Some of our pupils, those with SEN, have very particular learning needs. However, the more we can teach to the broad spectrum of learning the less we will have to make specific, special accommodations for pupils. The need will not have gone away, it is simply that more pupils will be engaged with learning for more of the time. Computers are powerful tools for making this possible.

2

Including all learners

There has been a shift in recent years from a narrow focus on SEN to a broader one on inclusion. This means meeting the individual learning needs not just of those with special needs, but of all pupils. This chapter will consider some of the different groups the term has come to cover, including those who are learning English as an additional language (EAL) and the gifted and talented.

Special education needs

Computers can offer access to the curriculum for SEN pupils in ways that other tools for learning cannot. There are two main ways to enable this. We can either change how the computer works, or we can add to it in some way. This is true for both hardware and software.

Changing what you've got

All computers have a set of programs installed known as the 'operating system' (OS). Whether you are using a Microsoft Windows based computer (commonly referred to as a PC), an Apple Macintosh machine, or a computer using open source software (this is software that is free to download and use) such as Linux, you will find that built into the machines are ways to change how they look, how we can input information and how they respond to what we do. Typically these include reading text out from the screen, changing the colour settings to get better contrasts, enlarging icons and fonts or providing magnification, and working with other means of control such as our voices or alternative hardware to the keyboard.

There are a number of ways of finding out what accessibility options are on offer for the computer operating system that you are using. One of the simplest ways is to use the Help files, easily found by pressing **F1** when you are on the desktop, then searching for 'Accessibility Options'. Although, while every operating system has adaptations that offer support to users with a variety of needs, due to security controls they sometimes need the help of a technician to set them up, particularly on networks. This means that even if you know how you want the computer to be adapted you may find you need to get help in order to make these changes. (In the National Occupational Standards there are several references to making sure children can access learning and that computers are adapted to their needs [STL 7.1 P3,5 and K18,19,22,24; STL 8.1 P3,4,6,7 and K11,12].)

Ease of Access Center

Microsoft Windows, the most commonly used operating system, provides a number of ways of adapting the machine to the needs of the individual, and a variety of routes to finding them – and to turning them on and off – including through the use of shortcuts. If you have not used these before, the best place to start is probably the 'Ease of Access Center'. From the **Start** button click on **All Programs** and then **Accessories**, and from there, select **Ease of Access**. Another way of finding this is to right click on the desktop and choose the **Personalize** option, which has a link directly to **Ease of Access**. And it can also be found in the Control Panel: again click on the **Start** button, then choose **Control Panel** and find it there. However, the quickest route is to hold down the **Start** key and then press **U** on the keyboard.

Once open a number of choices are available. The four most common tools are presented for immediate use, so you can **Start Magnifier**, **Start Narrator**, **Start On–Screen Keyboard** or **Set up High Contrast**. These are pretty much as they sound.

- Magnifier is a tool that enlarges areas of the screen as the mouse moves over them. It can enlarge up to 16 times the normal resolution, and can be set up either to follow the mouse or cover a particular portion of the screen.

- Narrator is a basic screen reader that will describe aloud the user's actions on the keyboard – so that they know what keys they have pressed – and will read the contents of dialog boxes and also the text of open pages on screen.

- On-Screen Keyboard is just that. It is designed for people who have difficulty pressing the keys, but who can control the cursor, either by using the mouse or through another pointing device, such as a joystick or eye-tracking system. The version in Windows 7 includes a text prediction feature to speed up input.

- High Contrast changes the appearance to make it easier to read the screen, typically by providing a black background with high visibility text, often yellow or white. It also enlarges the size of icons on the desktop and toolbars.

As well as these immediate adjustments further options are given. One possibility is to click on the offered help: 'Not sure where to start? Get recommendations to make your computer easier to use'. This then opens up a series of screens that ask questions about the user's access needs and ends with providing suggestions for settings.

The first of these pages is for eyesight and asks about lighting conditions, images on screens and whether a person is blind or has another kind of visual impairment. From here it goes on to ask about dexterity – whether it is hard to hold a pen or pencil, if the user has a physical condition affecting their arms or wrists or even whether they use a keyboard at all.

Following these, questions are asked about hearing and if conversations are hard to follow or background noises are distracting, and directly asking whether the user is deaf or hard of hearing. It goes on to ask about speech impediments, and next if there are cognitive difficulties such as with concentration or memory, or whether the user is possibly dyslexic or has another similar condition.

Once this short questionnaire is completed the computer will recommend which of the accessibility options the user might find helpful and gives the option to turn these on. Throughout the process the computer will also make the user aware of any additional software that has been installed on the machine that may be useful.

In some cases it might be clear from the beginning just what sorts of support the user needs and further help can be found by clicking on one of the options that follow further down the initial dialogue box. 'Use the computer without a display', will help to turn on Narrator and set up Text to Speech, a feature that allows users to control the computer by voice and to dictate documents, emails, web addresses and so on.

Under the 'Make the computer easier to see' link are suggestions again for Narrator, but also for high contrast, for the magnifier, and changes in the settings to use larger icons and text.

If the computer is to be set up to, 'Use the computer without mouse or keyboard', then suggestions are made to use the onscreen keyboard with a pointing device, or to use Speech Recognition.

It is also possible to 'Make the mouse easier to use', this includes changing the appearance of the cursor, using **Mouse Keys** – a feature whereby the mouse is controlled by the numeric keypad – or changing other features, such as: swapping the buttons over for left-handed use; adding a tail to the pointer to make it easier to see; changing the speed at which it moves across the screen; and initiating a feature whereby the pointer is circled on screen if the user presses the Ctrl key. All of these features are also available through the Control Panel.

Included in the 'Make the keyboard easier to use' list are, again, turning on the Mouse Keys, but also features to enable the mouse to be used more slowly, or one-handed. These features include **Sticky Keys**, which enables actions that require multiple key presses – such as using Shift to insert a capital letter, or shortcuts such as **Ctrl + P** to print – to be enacted as a series of presses instead of simultaneously, which can be very helpful for one-handed users. Then there is the **Toggle Keys** function, which makes a sound when you turn on keys that lock the keyboard in a certain state, such as **Caps Lock**, **Num Lock** or **Scroll Lock**. And finally there is the **Filter Keys** function, which slows the repeat rate on the keyboard down, meaning that if you hold a key down, the delay is lengthened so that you do not get lots of repeated letters – this is intended for people who find it difficult to lift their fingers quickly.

The option to use 'Text or visual alternatives for sounds' means that when a user would normally hear a system noise – a 'ping' of some sort – a visual cue will be given instead, such as flashing the open window.

Finally, there are suggestions to 'Make it easier to focus on tasks'. These offer several of the previously mentioned supports, including using the **Narrator**, **Sticky Keys**, **Toggle Keys** and **Filter Keys**, and it offers to turn off 'unnecessary animations when possible'.

Many of these features can be turned on quickly and automatically using keyboard shortcuts. As already mentioned, to get to the Ease of Access Center, **Windows key + U** can be used. High contrast can be activated by pressing **Alt + right Shift key + Print Screen**. Other features, such as **Filter Keys** can be activated by holding down the **left Shift key** for eight seconds.

Personalise

Also available is the option to **Personalise** the machine. Sounds and Mouse Pointers can be changed here, but this also gives access to the 'Window Color and Appearance' settings. These allow you to customise the colour scheme of documents, dialog boxes and windows. Choosing the **Advanced** button opens up a fresh, although similar looking, dialog box. Here you can click on the area you want to change and amend the colour combinations. For instance, by clicking on the Active Window you can change the background colour to cream and the text colour to dark blue, a variation that many dyslexics find easier to cope with. Once selected, any folders or documents that are opened, whether word-processing, spreadsheet, or presentation, will use those colours on screen without affecting the print outs.

Keyboard shortcuts

As mentioned previously, one of the quickest ways to get a computer to do something is through the use of keyboard shortcuts – that is, by pressing combinations of keys actions can be made to happen. For instance, holding down **Alt** while tapping the **Tab** key flicks through the open documents on a computer, and holding down **Ctrl** while turning the **scroll wheel** on the mouse changes the text size, and hence the magnification, on screen. When working with documents, **Ctrl + P** will bring up the print dialog box, **Ctrl + A** will select all the text, and **Ctrl + S** will save the document. While there are occasional variations, most of these are standard across all applications. They are useful for people who find using a mouse difficult, they are a quicker way to work and they can simplify processes. They also give the user the look of an expert as their fingers trot across the keyboard making things happen almost magically.

You can find keyboard shortcuts in a number of ways. In the first place, many menus include them alongside the commands they operate. If you open the Edit menu for instance (itself subject to the shortcut **Alt + E**) you will see a number of the functions have them. **Ctrl + Z** is the very useful **Undo** command (much quicker than taking your hand off the keyboard to find the mouse and manoeuvre the cursor to the icon). Alternatively, you can open the **Help** menu (**F1**) and search for 'Keyboard Shortcuts'.

These kinds of controls will probably be most useful when using a word processor such as MS Word, which also offers a couple of other options to make the program more useable.

One is the ability to set the default font and size when you open a document. Whenever you change the font attributes using the dialog box there is a button visible marked **Default**. Click this and every new document will use your current choices – very helpful for pupils with a range of difficulties, including dyslexia and visual impairments.

Also within word processors is the ability to create templates. These are documents that provide a readymade layout for users to complete. This could be a plan to write up an investigation, comprehension questions, or a even a cloze procedure. It can cut down the keyboarding a pupil needs to do and provide a structure with which to work. To make a template, simply create the document you want the pupils to use, then when you save it, choose 'Word Template' from the list that comes up.

One other feature of MS Word (and other word processors) is **Autocorrect**. This is the software's ability to put right typos and misspellings automatically. So, when you type 'teh' it magically becomes 'the'. This in itself is helpful for many pupils (although if you are trying to teach particular spellings you may want to turn it off). However, the Autocorrect can also be taught particular words, or even phrases, that can be dropped into a document with a couple of keystrokes. For instance, a child's initials can be replaced by their full name, or even a full address can be typed automatically. To do this, type the word or phrase you want to use into a document then highlight it. Next click on the **Office Button** (in the top left-hand corner) and choose **Word Options**, then **Proofing**, then **AutoCorrect Options**. Here the selected text should already be in place in the list of corrections, awaiting a short cut. For an address this could be, for instance, 'ad1'. On entering this sequence of keys and pressing the space bar the full address will appear.

Adding to what you've got

Although the tools built in to computers are very useful for many users, they are limited in what they do, so quite often pupils with special educational needs will require additional resources. This can be accomplished through installing more software, or connecting additional hardware, or both. The latter generally makes physical access easier, the former can also make tasks easier.

A desktop computer is ordinarily set up with a keyboard, a monitor and a mouse, and a laptop has them built in, but we can change or supplement any of these to make the machine easier to use. We could, for instance, add a larger monitor so that the screen is easier to see. For some pupils with visual impairments, however, even this may not help, as their field of vision may be limited to a small area and what we need to change is their seating so they can get closer.

Another adaptation would be to use a touch screen monitor. As the name suggests, these are activated by touching. The use of this technology is becoming very common, when buying rail or tube tickets, for instance, or as information points in museums, or self-service checkouts in supermarkets. They also come in many sizes: interactive whiteboards are oversized touch screens, and iPods and iPhones are examples of miniature ones; iPads and tablet PCs use touch screens combining both portability and visibility.

Apart from the adjustments to the keyboards response – **Toggle Keys** and **Filter Keys**, as mentioned previously – the most straightforward adaptation is to add a key guard. This is a sheet of pressed metal or plastic with finger sized holes drilled into it to that clips over a standard keyboard. This is for users with poor motor control so that they can run their hand over the guard then press down through the hole to select a key, preventing them from making multiple presses.

Keyboards

Alternative keyboards come in several forms – including layout. The QWERTY design came into being to keep the most used keys well apart in order to prevent manual typewriters from jamming. This means that it is not the fastest, nor the most user-friendly layout. Since then, other configurations have been promoted, with Dvorak being the best known, but these have not been adopted due to the cost of moving from one layout to another. However, most computer operating systems have these alternative designs available.

If it is necessary to change the keyboard itself, there are plenty of variations available. Some are designed with bigger keys that are easier to find and to see. They come in various formats – upper or lower case; QWERTY or alphabetical; black on white or coloured keys – and will also take a key guard. Others change the shape, so that the keyboard is no longer flat. One variation is a keyboard of two concave halves, which is designed to be more ergonomic than a flat one, thereby reducing repetitive strain injury (RSI), and this should be easier to use for longer periods by people with physical disabilities or weaknesses in their wrists.

Specialised keyboards for one-handed use are also concave, and are either left or right side specific. Again the design is intended to reduce unnecessary and unnatural movements. Some keyboards are split in the middle, with a universal joint at the top so the two halves are connected but can be moved relative to each other for users whose disabilities require specific positioning.

Other possibilities for users with limited movements are to use a mini keyboard, such as you might find on a laptop, or a chording keyboard. This latter has very few keys, typically nine, which are pressed in combinations to create letters. This can be a very fast process and can be used with one hand.

Another variation is the concept keyboard, one of the most popular of which is Intellikeys. This has a flat surface that can be angled on which overlays can be inserted. In some ways the concept keyboard is not a direct replacement for the standard keyboard as it can also be used to control any element of the computer, such as the mouse, and is therefore not just for writing text. The overlays may look like a standard keyboard, or just have arrows to drive the mouse, or may even be specially constructed to look like the software on screen. They are operated by pressing with a finger or a pointing device and can be positioned for optimal control by the user, with the overlays changed simply by slipping one out and another in. A barcode reader on the back tells the computer which one is in use.

Mouse

Alternatives to the standard mouse generally work by turning it upside down. Instead of moving the mouse around the table, with this moving the cursor on the screen, the process is reversed. The mouse stays still and the user manipulates a ball, or joystick. These devices come in several shapes and sizes, from desktop varieties to those that are designed to be worn on the index finger and controlled with the thumb. It is also possible to get touchpads, like those found on laptops, for users who can glide a finger over a surface.

Switches

Apart from the above devices that are variations on the ways we already use computers, there are other hardware adaptations that can require us to think differently about how we operate a computer. A commonly used device is the 'switch', which quite often looks similar to a button. These devices vary in sophistication both in their design and their use. The basis of it is that by hitting the switch an action occurs – rather like switching the lights on and off. Some users will be learning cause and effect – that the action causes a pattern to build on screen perhaps. Others will be using one or more switches in various ways to select letters and words to build up texts or to control their computers. The means of activating a switch can also vary, from a simple hit of a button to ones that are squeezed, flicked or rolled, depending on what the user finds easiest to do, and activation can be with the hand, but also with the foot, the head, the knee or any body part that has an assured, controlled movement. The system used by Professor Stephen Hawking to speak and to write his books is essentially a switch driven one, although driven by his sucking and puffing on a straw.

In operation, switches often require a control box to connect them, although some connect to the keyboard and others to the mouse. They can work as the left and right mouse buttons, the Enter key or space bar, or specific keys for particular functions, such as opening the internet.

Switches can also be used with varying degrees of complexity to work communication aids. These can vary from a single button with a pre-recorded message, such as 'Here, Miss', to be used at registration, through to rows of messages to be worked with a direct press or through scanning with a switch, to those that have several levels and allow users to hold complex conversations.

Assessment

When considering specialist hardware and software for pupils, your school may want to enlist the services of a range of professionals. Some local authorities have advisors specially trained in this work, or will request an assessment from an external expert. Speech therapists will be called on when there is a communication aid under consideration, as well as occupational and physiotherapists who will advise on positioning and mounting requirements. In many instances, common sense will guide you; however, it will be as well to ask an expert as some aspects of the use of devices can lead to longer term problems if you do not get it right initially.

Specialist software

Adaptations involving specialist software can either be to support additional hardware, or they can simply run on a standard set up. Some hardware will not run without having its own drivers installed, or it may require particular programs to help pupils to learn to use it.

Switch users, for instance, may need especially designed programs in order to get the hang of how the devices work. These might be a straightforward sequence that builds a pattern, as in Switch It! Patterns, or a familiar object, as in Switch It! Diggers. At the initial level, each hit of the button adds the next layer, with a progression that requires the buttons to be touched alternately. Other titles, such as Choose It Maker, are designed for switch use and the teaching of concepts such as sequencing, or learning about difference through identifying an image as the odd one out.

A more advanced use is to write, or draw, with switches, both of which are possible through the use of Clicker 5. This popular program originated with switch users in mind, providing an onscreen keyboard that could be driven by one or two switches. From this simple premise a much more powerful program has grown that now has a painting version. Here users drive the cursor around hotspots on the screen to add colour or stamps of images. Sophisticated use can lead to drawing independently.

For pupils learning to use touch screens or tracker balls, painting programs are a useful starting point as they give immediate results and will work in a similar way to working on paper. Some, such as RM's Colour Magic, also have sounds built in as an additional hook. Very useful for getting users engaged with touch screens, or interactive whiteboards, are titles such as Pretty Things and Noisy Things, both of which are wonderfully engaging and, although initially designed for children in early years settings, work very well for those with a range of special educational needs at all ages (and as a distraction for their teachers!).

Keyboarding

Pupils who rely on keyboards will benefit from learning how to use them properly – in fact, all pupils would be better off if trained to type correctly. Unfortunately, while touch typing is a highly desirable skill, the constraints of the timetable and the fact that this can be a tedious pursuit might prevent it happening. (Although the same could be said of handwriting, and we have no qualms about asking young children to have daily practice at that.)

Touch typing reduces problems such as RSI, and it also increases productivity – in both quantity and quality – and frees up the mind to focus on the work rather than on finding the correct keys. There are some programs that have been designed especially for young people to learn to type, which usually include other educational aspects such as spelling. For example, Type to Learn tries to strike a balance between the repetitiveness of learning and the use of games to brighten things up, while using common words and letter groupings as practice drills. Even programs such as 2Type, which aims to increase keyboard awareness rather than teach touch typing, would benefit children. There are also some free resources online, the BBC's being the best of these. Finally, specialist programs, such as Five Fingered Typist, are available for those who can only use one hand.

It is known that developing a motor memory of how words are spelled can help pupils with literacy difficulties or dyslexia. By regularly building words on a keyboard, the movement of fingers helps pupils to remember how to spell these words. This is recognised in First Keys to Literacy, which teaches children initial letter sounds and simple spellings alongside keyboard awareness.

Supports for writing

While typing ability will be a useful skill for children when creating texts in schools, there are lots of other ways in which computers can become more supportive for this purpose, some of which are becoming part of everyone's toolkits. As discussed previously, dictation software is now quite common, being available in the most recent Windows operating systems.

There is also prediction software, which we are all familiar with from creating messages on our mobile phones – as the user's thumbs tap away so suggestions are made as to the word they may be wanting to use. Computer versions, such as Penfriend and Co:Writer, work in a similar way. The user types in the first letter and a list of words appears. If the desired one is not there, they can add another letter and so on until the word they want appears – or does not. Although, even then these programs are capable of learning new words and adding them to the store of those available ready for the next time, so new words, for the latest topic perhaps, can be pre-loaded. These programs work on the sense of a sentence, so they will predict the next word even before a letter is pressed, particularly as they learn a user's style. Selection of the desired word can be in one of several ways: by using the mouse; by pressing a number; by choosing a function key from the top of the keyboard; and even by the use of a switch.

Predictive software is useful for pupils who have difficulty spelling, and for those with motor control difficulties. The former group only need to begin to spell the word and then pick it out from a list, whereas for the latter group the software reduces the number of keystrokes necessary to write any word. As mentioned, the predictor will often suggest the next word without any letters being typed, this can mean writing a whole sentence by choosing each word with one click of the mouse.

Another common support for pupils when writing is the use of word grids. These can provide individual words, phrases or whole sentences that can be added to the text by the click of a mouse or by pressing a switch. There are specialist programs for this, the most well known of which is the aforementioned Clicker 5 and its variant for secondary pupils, Wordbar.

The advantage of using programs with word grids is that support can be given to pupils in different ways at several levels, either as key vocabulary for a task; as sections of text that can be built into varied sentences; or as whole sentences to be placed in the correct sequence.

Clicker 5 provides several tools that will support writing. It can be set up to be simply a talking word processor with several speech options. At letter level this can be useful to visually impaired typists who need to know that they are typing accurately. However, as it is the letter name rather than the sound that is given, it is of limited value for those starting to learn to spell.

At word level the computer will read the input phonetically, so 'kow' or 'kat' will sound correct even though they are not, and words with unconventional spellings, or names such as Siobhan, will be pronounced incorrectly. However, the program also has a bank of graphics built in, so if a word is correctly spelled an image will appear. As users can add their own images, this is helpful for children learning to spell their names, for instance, as whenever they get it right their photo appears. Symbol banks can also be added to be inserted automatically in order to help with reading and writing. Finally, when the computer is set to read the whole sentence as punctuation is added, the user will be able hear if what they have written makes sense, if the words are in the right order and if any have been missed out.

Clicker 5 also comes with an onscreen keyboard, which is designed to work with switches (as described above). The writing grids will also work in this way, so children can create whole texts through given sentences and phrases, or sequence a known text, access a personalised vocabulary book and even create their own talking books, with options to add both images and text to a prepared template. While originating in the special needs field, the software is sufficiently flexible for it to be used by pupils of all abilities, including providing the challenge for higher ability students to create multimedia books and presentations in a format that can be posted on the internet.

Screen readers

Not only are talking word processors such as Clicker 5 – or other examples such as Talking First Word or Write Outloud – helpful for creating text, but they can also be used to read out passages of text that are opened up within them. However, there are also programs specifically designed to perform this function, known as 'screen readers', and they perform exactly that function. Screen Reader is one such program, although there are several that are free to download from the internet.

Some applications that provide screen reading functionality also provide other supports. Both Texthelp Read and Write and Claro Suite work as screen readers, but they also act as 'bolt-on' talking word processors and have predictive text capabilities. They will also provide talking dictionaries and homophone checkers.

Symbols

Another support for both reading and writing is the use of symbols. These are similar in a way to the use of other graphics and images; however, as well as representing concrete objects and actions, such as 'pizza' or 'eating lunch', symbols also encompass abstract ideas such as 'enjoyment' or 'taste'. When children first learn to read from picture books they will look at all the information on a page, both the text and the images, to help with decoding. Symbols work in a similar way, although instead of giving a general idea about what is happening they can appear alongside key vocabulary to help with specific meanings.

The most widely used programs for working with symbols are produced by Widgit, so its titles are often referred to as such, rather than by their correct names. Widgit's two most popular outputs are Communicate:Inprint and Communicate:SymWriter. The first of these is designed as a symbolised desktop publisher, with the outputs usually being printouts for such things as storybooks, visual timetables and overlays for communication aids. The second is a word processor that adds symbols to text to help with writing, ensuring that a word is the correct one and that the sentence makes sense.

There is more than one set of symbols available to be used with such programs – as well as the Rebus symbols that Widgit mainly uses for its software, there are others such as Makaton and PCS Mayer-Johnson. This latter is the main set used with Boardmaker software. While similar to Communicate:Inprint, this is mainly for creating printed products such as overlays for communication aids and visual timetables, and it can also be used to make onscreen activities for pupils.

Another activity that supports children's learning is creating mind maps. These are recognised as a support for both understanding and remembering, and also for structuring other pieces of work, such as texts or presentations. Communicate:Ideas is a symbol version of this, with colour-coded branches that can be hidden or revealed, and symbols and graphics available to reinforce the content of each box. Most mind-mapping programs, including 2Connect and Inspiration, also encourage the use of graphics in the map.

Widgit has also produced symbol software to make the internet more accessible by providing an online glossary. With Widgit's Point a user hovers on a word so the appropriate symbol (or choice of symbols if more than one interpretation is possible) pops up with a written definition. Similarly, Insite will create symbolic illustrations of pages of text for web developers to post.

Speech control

There are other specialist titles available to be used for both controlling a computer by using assistive technology, such as switches, and for making it into a voice output communication aid (VOCA). One popular example is The Grid2, which is very flexible and can be used by pupils of all abilities, but is particularly useful for those who have restricted mobility, even to the point of controlling all the functions of a computer, from turning it on to shutting it down.

This level of control is also available from some of the more sophisticated speech recognition programs such as Dragon Dictate. As well as writing text, the user can give commands including opening programs, formatting text, saving and printing. As they have developed so these programs have become more reliable and are now considered to be as accurate as typing. The only drawback is that users currently need to have a reasonable reading ability to be able to recognise and correct any wrong words the computer types should it misunderstand what is said. Although the software has a speech feedback facility, so users can hear back what they have said, unless they know the correct spelling of a word they may not be able to put it right. The other issue is that speech-to-text only takes away the need to use a mouse and a keyboard – pupils still have to know what it is they want to write.

Visual impairment

Other specialist software available includes more sophisticated magnifiers and screen readers, such as Jaws. Jaws is specifically for visually impaired students and gives both control over magnification, contrast, brightness and so on, but also the speed at which text can be read. People who are blind or severely visually impaired can be quite adept at receiving information aurally, more so than sighted people, so will often play audio significantly faster. There are also specialist audio players designed for the blind that use a system called Daisy. This not only has variable speed, but also enables users to bookmark where they got to in a talking book. With the increased use of the internet, these resources are often in a downloadable format, rather than on a physical CD or DVD.

Working online

The internet has also seen a shift where programs are no longer on our computers, but run online, so as well as using the web for finding information and resources, we can also create and share our own outputs. Crick Software, the creators of the Clicker 5 titles, have also produced Write Online. This works as a word processor, and it can have text and screen colours changed and fonts enlarged to suit user's access needs, but it also has speech feedback, prediction and word grids available, so they can get as much, or as little, support as they require. It even has a mind-mapping facility built in to help with planning. As it is on the web, these features are available to students whenever and wherever they can get connected.

The future

The use of ICT to ameliorate SEN continues to develop, with many steps bringing the possibility of thought control closer. It is already possible to control the mouse through pads attached to the forehead that pick up minute electrical impulses. Beyond this, it is possible to wire the nervous system directly into a machine, and there is work in the United States on using the power of thought to control the computer directly. All the time, the gap between the machine and the brain is narrowing, and the closer the link the greater will be the possibilities for users with SEN to exploit the power of the technology.

Mobile phones and iPods are now able to act as talking communication aids, making a common tool into a very powerful one for people without speech. These devices are also proving useful for the blind as GPS systems, like those used in cars, to provide guidance as they walk the streets. Similarly they can provide on-the-spot information to people with learning difficulties, including directions and instructions to help them carry out everyday tasks. Applications for handheld devices now include ones whereby a photo can be taken of a piece of text, and the software will then read the text, even translating it. And functioning as pocket-sized translation machines means that they are helpful to the next category to be considered, those who are learning English as an additional language.

Supporting pupils for whom English is an additional language

Pupils who are learning English in addition to their mother tongue will be learning to read and write the language, as well as to speak it. For them, ICT can offer help in many ways, and several of the approaches used with those with special needs are similarly applicable to this group. Symbols supporting text can give an added visual prompt. Word banks can help with structuring writing and predictors with getting something down accurately. Screen readers will help by reading to students as they follow a text.

Spoken transcripts of given texts can also be created. There are several ways to do this. One is for teachers to record them for students and to save them in a format that can be used on an iPod or MP3 player. Another is to use software to do this. Both Claroread and Texthelp Read and Write have facilities not only to read the screen, but also to convert it into an audio file that can be copied onto a portable audio device – an iPod or MP3 player, for instance.

Another useful tool is the use of cloze exercises, where words are missed out of a text for pupils to complete. Programs such as Developing Tray or Clozepro help to develop literacy skills by challenging pupils to find missing words using the cues available, such as the meaning of the sentence or the part of speech that is missing. In the latter, a reading passage is created and pupils fill in missing words; however, a number of supports are available, such as word grids, shadows of the missing word and 'quick peeks'.

Online tools

Translation is now a very common tool online. The Google search page, for instance, has a 'language tools' link that will not only translate text between many languages, but also search in different languages, or set up the browser to work in one particular language. Some browsers, such as Google's Chrome, will offer to translate pages as you arrive on them.

Then there is Voki. This website creates an avatar for you that can then be used to practice foreign languages by typing in text, then selecting a language and hearing the avatar say it for you. A discrete, but good, fun way to translate written text into spoken words and to understand pronunciation.

With the increased capacities of mobile phones and the ability of devices to capture images and convert the text in the image into speech, handheld machines are opening up the possibilities for understanding and exploring language. It is believed that simultaneous translation of spoken language will soon be possible, so a person making a phone call will be able to talk to anyone in the world, with the device making sure each can understand the other. Despite this, learning the language of the culture within which you live will remain an important route to inclusion, as it offers insights into a society that technology alone cannot give.

Gifted and talented pupils

This group of pupils often explore the ICT on offer simply to see what it will do, and to see if they can make it do something it shouldn't. Such energies need to be directed into creative tasks. Computers can offer both more challenging tasks and more challenge in how they are completed.

Providing a challenge

There are many ways in which ICT can be used to extend tasks. Excel, for instance, can be used in maths to explore complex calculations and to look for patterns, or to draw graphs of mathematical expressions.

Using MS Word can present a number of challenges. The Word Count facility can be used to challenge pupils to write to a specific length. Tasks might include to create a complete story in exactly 100 words, or retell a Shakespeare play in exactly 50 words. The Thesaurus tool offers the opportunity to explore using alternative words in a sentence to see how the sense of it changes, for instance changing 'walked' to 'ambled' or 'paced', or maybe 'smiled' to 'smirked' or 'beamed'.

The use of some software can lead these pupils to create their own challenges in learning how it works. PowerPoint, for instance, has many variations of animations and transitions. The presentations themselves can offer pupils opportunities to show their skills through the complexity of what they produce. Other tasks, such as creating web pages, in themselves can be quite demanding. And programs such as Logo (this was specifically designed for exploratory, constructivist, learning) are open ended in the degree of challenge available, from creating sequences of squares to having the turtle write the pupil's name in joined up writing, all the time with the pupil programming and creating procedures.

Students can also create and share computer games, using programs such as Scratch. This can be downloaded to make different sorts of platform games, or multimedia creations, with the results uploaded for others to share.

Working online

Schools are increasingly creating their own online presence, particularly through the use of a 'learning platform' (see Chapter 9 for more on this). This is a set of tools that allow teachers to create lessons to use in class, which students can then access later for revision and homework purposes. Learning platforms also include communication facilities, such as message boards, and will link to management information systems for staff to update mark books and even for parents to sign in to see how their offspring are doing. There are possibilities for staff to provide work tailored to each child's interests and level at which they are working, for them to do things at their own pace, and even in their own time and place.

The internet also offers the opportunity to share ideas and voice opinions through wikis and blogs. The first of these refers to information sites that many users contribute to, the most widely known example being Wikipedia, where anyone can create a page, and any other user can edit it — although there are controls in place for people to challenge each other's entries and updates. Blogs are simply online diaries, supplemented recently by vlogs — video diaries. As well as these possibilities, podcasts are becoming more common. These can be thought of as online radio programmes, sometimes with accompanying images.

Information online

Original census data is now online, a rich, primary source for studying history, geography, statistics, sociology, economics and politics at many levels. Google Earth, Streetview and Multimap give us different perspectives on where we live and the wider world, letting us see it from above, or overlaid with information, virtually travelling along streets and visiting remote places, many previously beyond our reach. Photos and film of historic events, scientific advances and faraway places, such as Mars, are easily available. The images from the Hubble Telescope or those sent back to NASA from the orbiting space station are good examples of this.

The use of webcams allows us to both receive information and to give it out. There are cameras pointed at streets in towns, nesting boxes in woods and watering holes around the world for us to see animals in their natural habitat. (Although there are times when nothing will be seen because animals often water at dawn and dusk when people are not in school. A valuable lesson in itself.)

Videoconferencing

Webcams also offer videoconferencing, using professional equipment or free, online services such as Skype or MSN. The quality of the camera may produce images of variable quality, but there is still the opportunity to see and talk to someone in a remote place who we may not be able to contact otherwise. This could be an expert, an archaeologist perhaps to discuss an excavation, or another child, maybe one who uses sign language to communicate, to create a richer learning experience. Webcams offer the chance for schools across a wide geographical area to connect with students, sharing experiences. One such project links the Shetland Islands to South Africa for a Higher Level course on the apartheid system.

The Global Leap website is a site that links up schools with providers of video conferences to give learning experiences that were hitherto impossible.

Can computers replace teachers?

There has been discussion about how such uses of ICT will change classrooms, so that pupils can be supervised by teaching assistants while being taught from afar by subject experts. While this might seem attractive, the richest learning experiences arise from educational professionals working alongside pupils to tailor learning to the needs of individuals and groups. ICT can truly enrich learning and enhance educational opportunities for pupils, regardless of their individual learning needs.

The range of hardware and software available might seem daunting, and it would be very difficult to understand how to use it all. It is therefore better to know a handful of programs well and use them effectively than to know a little about a lot. Focus on being able to find and use appropriate software for the pupils you work with for the tasks they need to complete [STL 7.2 P2,3,4 and K1,14,15,16,17,18,20,21; STL 8.1 P3,4,5,6,7; STL 8.2 P3,4,5,6,7,8 and K2,3,4,11,12,14,25].

3

Using ICT in teaching and learning

The terms IT (information technology) and ICT (information and communication technology) are often used interchangeably, although the latter term is little known outside of education. Generally schools think of IT as being the technology, the equipment and the infrastructure, and ICT as what we do with it, the subject and the way it is used to support learning. Sometimes the term is pluralised, 'information and communication technologies', as there are now a number of different tools, devices, functions and possibilities that ICT covers – a range that continues to grow and diversify.

We no longer think of ICT simply as desktop computers, nor of computing in schools as learning to use office software to create letters and posters, databases and emails. New technologies are now thought much more of as tools for communicating, for receiving information from every place across the planet, and of transmitting it too. We now connect with millions of people in diverse places, tell them who we are and share our ideas and interests.

In schools ICT is both a curriculum subject and a tool for learning in other subjects, an academic discipline and a 'service subject' – like handwriting – one that enables learning. The skills learned in ICT lessons are put into practice across the rest of the timetable, not only because it is good practice, but because it is a statutory requirement. Learning about, and with, ICT is compulsory and is laid down as such in the National Curriculum [STL 8 K21].

The National Curriculum

There are common themes across all age groups in the ICT National Curriculum, which was originally introduced in 1988 and has since been revised. The current primary curriculum has been in place since 1999, while a new secondary curriculum was introduced in 2008 [STL 8 K4]. As with English and maths, ICT is a 'core' curriculum subject – that is, all children in all phases of education are expected to study it, although it does not have to be taught as a discrete subject. It can be taught through other subjects, which is often the case in KS4, when students will have many skills that are then applied in a more focused way within the subjects they have chosen.

Primary ICT curriculum

In primary schools, in common with other subjects, the National Curriculum breaks ICT down into several strands under two common headings, 'Knowledge, Skills and Understanding' and 'Breadth of Study'. The first of these is what children should learn, the latter the learning experiences they should encounter in the process.

The ICT curriculum has four aspects:

- Finding things out – This means knowing how to find information and verify, evaluate, analyse and assess it, and make sense of what it means.

- Developing ideas and making things happen – This requires pupils to bring different ideas together to develop and refine them, giving instructions and monitoring what happens, and to use ICT to explore situations, asking 'what if?' questions.

- Exchanging and sharing information – This is about sharing information in a variety of ways, and thinking about the way it is provided and the needs of the intended audience.

- Reviewing, modifying and evaluating work as it progresses – This means that pupils will think about what they are doing and how ICT benefits them.

All of these are underpinned by the Breadth of Study, which is about ensuring that pupils are given a range of different experiences with ICT and think about its impact on their lives and the wider society.

These broad aims are consistent throughout a pupil's schooling, although presented differently in the secondary curriculum. There is a statutory requirement to use ICT in teaching and learning in all other subjects, with some exceptions in KS1, such as physical education (PE).

While the National Curriculum determines what should be taught, how this happens is up to schools. To help them with their planning the Qualifications and Curriculum Authority (QCA, subsequently changed to the QCDA with the addition of Development to its title) developed a scheme of work. Although it is not compulsory for schools to use this planning – and many local authorities and commercial organisations produce their own – it is expected that whatever schools do is at least up to the QCA's standard, if not better.

Secondary ICT curriculum

In secondary schools the Knowledge, Skills and Understanding is presented as a number of key concepts that need to be learned and understood:

- Capability – This is about using a variety of tools and applications to address questions and problems and to generate ideas and solutions 'of value', as well as using new technologies as they emerge, and transferring skills into other situations.

- Communication and collaboration – This explores the ways in which ICT enables us to share ideas and information with others across the world, working together, being creative and generating new knowledge.

- Exploring ideas and manipulating information – This focuses on problem solving, on modelling different scenarios and on dealing with large volumes of data.

- Impact of technology – This promotes thinking about how ICT has changed our lives, and will do so in the future, including social, ethical and cultural implications, as well as the need to be safe and responsible users of it.

- Critical evaluation – This asks students to think about the information they are presented with and to question its validity and usefulness, as well as reflecting on their own outputs.

There are then a number of key processes students need to grasp in order to make progress:

- Finding information – Doing this in an informed and critical way.

- Developing ideas – This requires using the right tools for problem solving, testing out hypotheses and exploring relationships, and bringing together different media to present information.

- Communicating information – This focuses on using different formats and ways of doing so, ensuring the methods they choose are fit for purpose and meet the needs of the audience.

- Evaluating – This ensures critical review of their own work, and of their peers, and requires reflecting on what they have learned.

As with the primary National Curriculum there is also a requirement, in the Range and Content, to ensure students encounter a breadth of technologies and are competent to work with aspects such as data security, online safety and respecting the rights of others. They also need to appreciate the impact of ICT on their lives and the wider society.

The statutory requirement to use ICT across all subjects remains, with expectations of students working collaboratively, sharing ideas and solving real-life problems, while selecting the most appropriate tools for the job – whether these tools are electronic or not. In every subject's National Curriculum requirements there is reference made to the role of ICT, with suggestions as to how this requirement can be fulfilled. In geography, for instance, a required 'Curriculum Opportunity' is to, 'investigate important issues of relevance to the UK and globally using a range of skills, including ICT' [STL 8 K21].

Assessment

Attainment targets

As well as providing a common educational entitlement for all children, the National Curriculum has a set of Attainment Targets to help determine what progress they are making and how far they have got. There are eight levels described, with one more level for exceptional performance. Each level progresses from the previous one, so common threads can be seen developing throughout. The descriptors lay out what achievement at a particular level consists of.

ICT at Level 3, for instance, is described as:

> Pupils use ICT to save information and to find and use appropriate stored information, following straightforward lines of enquiry. They use ICT to generate, develop, organise and present their work. They share and exchange their ideas with others. They use sequences of instructions to control devices and achieve specific outcomes. They make appropriate choices when using ICT-based models or simulations to help them find things out and solve problems. They describe their use of ICT and its use outside school.

Although it is recognised that every child progresses at their own rate, as with maths and English, most pupils are expected to be at Level 2 at the end of KS1, Level 4 at the end of KS2 and Level 5/6 at the end of KS3. Schools are expected to report a level at the end of each key stage, but previous to this, they will often simply state whether a child is working 'at', 'above' or 'below' the expected level for that year group.

P Scales

It is recognised that some children, because of their special educational needs, may not achieve at these levels throughout their school careers so the 'P' Scales were introduced to extend the Attainment Targets to accommodate them. Here 'P' stands for 'Pre' – that is, they are 'Pre' National Curriculum levels. There are eight levels on the P Scales. The first four levels are not subject specific (although they can be applied to each area of the curriculum) and largely relate to children's communication and response to the world around them.

The upper levels, P4–P8, become subject specific and progress into the standard National Curriculum levels. P8, for instance is as follows:

> Pupils find similar information in different formats, (a photo, in a paper, in a book, on a website, from a TV programme). Pupils use ICT to communicate and present their ideas. Pupils can load a resource and make a choice from it. They communicate about their use of ICT.

Progression

Progression between the levels can be seen by looking at the language used in the descriptor. The level that follows P8 is National Curriculum Level 1:

> Pupils explore information from various sources, showing they know that information exists in different forms. They use ICT to work with text, images and sound to help them share their ideas. They recognise that many everyday devices respond to signals and instructions. They make choices when using such devices to produce different outcomes. They talk about their use of ICT.

(Note: All the descriptors for both P Scales and National Curriculum Levels can be readily found on the internet.)

You can see that at P8, the lower level, children can 'find similar information in different formats', while at NC1, the next one up, they 'explore information from various sources, showing they know that information exists in different forms'. So, at P8 they only have to 'find' information, at NC1 they have to 'explore' it – that is, do something with it, ask questions of it, see what differences there are, be aware of various ways of presenting it – in print or electronically – and how these might be used for diverse reasons.

Similarly, at P8 they 'use ICT to present and communicate their ideas', while NC1 is more specific in that they will use ICT 'to work with text, images and sound', and at NC3 'to generate, develop, organise and present their work'. This progression could be from finding an image of something they like and talking about it, to labelling the image and printing it out, and on to using a number of images to show how something has changed over time, sequencing them and even adding a soundtrack. Alongside the development of ICT skills with each of these tasks is also the application of it to a task – thinking about the final outcome, the intended audience and what is the best way to achieve it.

Methods of assessment

When determining children's progress, teachers talk about two sorts of assessment, 'formative' and 'summative'. The first of these is ongoing: it is about looking at how far pupils have got and using this information in helping them to make more progress. The second happens at a particular point and is a measure of what a child knows and understands at that moment. In schools we use a combination of both, to help pupils as they work and to record what they have achieved at key points.

Summative assessment

Summative assessment is like a snapshot – it tells you where a child is at a certain point. GCSEs can be seen in this way as they give an indication of achievement at the end of KS4, and although they give a grade, they do not say what a child would need to do to get a better one. Similarly, we might see a spelling test as summative. Either the child does, or does not, know how to spell certain words. It is not diagnostic, it does not ascertain strategies used and how successful these were. It simply determines what is known at nine o'clock on a Monday morning.

Formative assessment

With formative assessment the approach is to consider how well a pupil is doing, then give them feedback and advice to help them progress further. It is less about determining where they are and more about providing guidance for where they could get to. This will help teaching staff, such as yourself, to appreciate how effective their instruction is, and what adjustments could make it more so. It will also help the pupils to take control of their own learning, to make their own decisions on how to improve their work and, thus, to progress accordingly.

Within ICT this might be a conversation in which questions are asked such as, 'You are at level 3. Can you think about who will look at your presentation? What will make it easier for them to understand?' By demonstrating a sense of audience, the work could be lifted to a level four.

Processes of assessment

Assessment takes place in different ways, both formal and informal, and at different times, with the method in part dependent on what the purpose is. To get a qualification, such as a GCSE, requires a formal assessment, including exams and coursework carried out in school time. But to gauge a child's degree of understanding in class may just be a case of asking them questions, or listening when they talk about their work to an adult or their peers.

Some assessments might be very specifically designed to assess abilities, such as a reading test or the Cognitive Ability Tests (CATs) that many secondary schools use for new entrants. Or they may be focused on particular areas of special educational needs, such as speech and language difficulties or dyslexia. Others may take the form of questioning a class at the end of the lesson to gauge levels of understanding quickly, with targeted questions for selected children at various points in the ability range for that group.

The assessment process draws on different evidence to come to a judgement. This will involve samples of work, both printed and onscreen – a picture, animation or website the child has created, for instance. However, these products alone do not say much about the process the pupil undertook to get to that point. To find out the reasons for the choices they made, the decisions they took and the things they learned as they went along requires other approaches. As mentioned, talking is one useful method, another is to ask them to keep a record themselves, perhaps as a blog, or to annotate a print out. They could also do a presentation, either to the whole class or a small group, or answer questions – perhaps in a 'hot-seat' situation.

The role of teaching assistants

While assessment is the responsibility of the class teacher, teaching assistants have an important role to play as well, as they often spend quite focused time with particular groups or individuals. They will have a better sense of what has happened during a lesson, whether the educational objectives have been met, and what learning a child has recently demonstrated and how. While a child may not have completed a piece of work, for instance, they might have shown insight through a comment they made that will only be noted if the teaching assistant makes sure it is recorded.

Teaching assistants are also often involved in formative assessment, possibly without knowing it. Their role in understanding the learning objectives – and in helping to achieve these – by modifying or differentiating them for particular children means that they are aware of the steps needed to get to a desired outcome. Along the way they will question children to see how much has been understood, then provide further guidance and input to help the child move on or change the activity or resources to make sure they remain engaged and learning [STL 8.2 P9,10].

Teaching assistants, therefore, have a great deal of information about how children are working. In passing this on to colleagues it can be helpful to understand and use the language of the assessment criteria. Reading the level descriptors is one way to do this, along with looking at the key vocabulary that is listed in the scheme of work or lesson plan. Think about whether a child has found information, or whether they have explored it. Maybe they have even gone so far as to organise it or been posed a question and decided what information they needed to find in order to answer it. This will help to ensure that you represent what a child has learned accurately and professionally and that they get due credit for what they have achieved. You may also want to have pieces of evidence available, or be able to quote specific instances of when a child has shown what they know. These could occur at any time a child is using ICT, in any curriculum area and not exclusively in ICT lessons [STL 7 K17,21; STL 8.1 P8; STL 8.2 P9,12 and K16,26].

Peer and self-assessment

Peer or self-assessment can take several forms. In the first, instance a child can be asked to evaluate their own work against the given criteria for it. For instance, if they have been asked to design an advert for an event they can critique whether the message is prominent enough, the format appropriate – including fonts, colours and styles, and the use of images – and whether it appeals to the intended audience. They could also think about the medium – whether it is a poster, flyer, email or web page.

They can critique their peers' work in a similar way. Because of the nature of the internet, digital work can be shared with, and evaluated by, pupils at another location (perhaps anonymously) very easily. Or a pupil might address the class, talking about the decisions made and the tools used, answering questions and receiving feedback (mainly positive) as they do. These arrangements can be formal or informal, structured or fairly loose. Whatever the situation, staff need to set up self and peer assessment carefully, making explicit what is expected in terms of both behaviour and criteria for levelling.

While it might be supposed that children would go easy on themselves, or see passing judgement on the work of classmates as an opportunity for settling scores, the reality is usually that they are harder on themselves than adults are and that they take the task seriously, offering helpful feedback and constructive criticism. The need to focus on what makes a good piece of work helps children to improve their own work, and critically evaluating others' sparks ideas for future projects.

Moderation

In order to make consistent judgements about pupil's work a process of moderation is helpful; this is where samples of work are compared across groups and ability ranges. Schools will often collect samples over a number of years to help ensure that levelling remains constant year on year. It will also help to make sure each child has a range of work to both ensure the breadth of the ICT curriculum is covered and to show progress over time. As ICT is in use across the curriculum, it will be possible to gather evidence of achievement, and work samples, from lessons other than ICT.

Target setting

As well as providing information about a pupil's progress, assessment is useful for target setting. Formative assessment looks to the future and gives guidance on what a pupil needs to do to progress further, whereas setting a target is a little different. Here progress is watched over a period of time, since starting school even, and consideration given to the rate at which a child is developing and what this means in terms of their future achievement. By looking at the course their progress is taking it is possible to make a reasonable judgement about future levels, and monitor their movement towards them.

Assessing pupil progress

One systematic approach to monitoring achievement is Assessing Pupil Progress (APP). This requires assessment at particular points through the year drawn from across the pupil's work and evaluated against an Assessment Focus (AF). In ICT, for instance, the AFs are 'Planning, developing and evaluating', 'Handling data, sequencing instructions and modelling' and 'Finding, using and communicating information'. While these are strands of the National Curriculum, the criteria for assessment, provided by the QCDA, are more nuanced than the Attainment Targets. Each pupil is considered against the level at which the teacher thinks they are most likely to be, and against one level above and one below. A judgement can then be made about not only what level the child is at, but also whereabouts within it they are – that is, whether they are low, secure, or high.

Conclusion

Assessment is an integral part of schooling; without it we do not know what has been learned, nor how well, and what has yet to be covered. It also helps inform our own practice, as part of pondering how well children are doing is about examining our own effectiveness. Is a failure to progress due to the challenge being too great for a child? Or is it because we have not found the best way to get learning across to them? It can be just as much an evaluation of our own practice as of a pupil's achievement and learning abilities. However, understanding how each has had an impact on the other can require us to be honest and self-critical, which will lead to our becoming better practitioners, and therefore provide a better education for the children.

The scope of ICT

Introduction

The pace of change of new technologies is becoming so accepted that we barely notice anymore. They are so much part of our lives that we do not remember a time when we did not have them and the ability to create, communicate, research, shop, share and collaborate in ways that were inconceivable until very recently. This chapter will pause to take stock of what those changes have been, think about how they have affected our work in schools and suggest what might be coming next.

The pace of change

The average handbag may well contain more computing power than the Apollo 11 capsule that first put astronauts on the moon. This was only forty years ago, but the personal computer was not invented then, not until the mid-1970s. Now we have a plethora of devices that continue to grow and develop, merging into gizmos with multiple uses, constantly becoming more powerful machines that can connect to the internet and to each other almost anywhere.

Once a single computer took up a room, then computers moved onto desks, then laps and now hands. The keyboard has been supplemented, and supplanted, by voice control, touch screens, and even eye gaze and thought control, with devices responding to multiple touches on the screen and changing orientation as they are moved around.

A tool for academics to make mind-boggling calculations became a way for office staff to streamline productivity, and it is now a mainstay of shopping, staying in touch with friends, watching films, listening to music, dating, doing business, banking, looking up information, completing schoolwork, paying our bills, and having our information stored and shifted around by central and local government and other agencies, such as the health service.

The technologies

People carry a lot of technology around with them – a mobile phone, an MP3 player, a USB memory key, a personal digital assistant (PDA – an electronic personal diary/organiser), a video camera and even a satnav (satellite navigation). Although, of course, it would be possible to carry all of these in one machine. Along with a voice recorder and note taker. And what with the many apps now available for pocket-sized devices, it could also be a spirit level, a translator, a drum kit, a compass, a stethoscope and even a means of finding out the name of a tune you are listening to, but can't quite remember what it is. Separate technologies for each of these still exist as well, and are often preferred for their better quality results and ease of use.

These devices are not the preserve of adults, with many children carrying phones and iPods wherever they go. They might also carry a games console, such as PlayStation Portable (PSP) or Nintendo DS. While at home they could be playing games on the computer, or just as likely on their Xbox or PlayStation 2 – all of which are capable of connecting to the internet to play online, sometimes with people they have not met face to face. Or they could also be used to browse the web and find information.

Even in nursery and early years classes there has been a growth in ICT, with many more devices for this age group, whether as toys for the role-play area, such as shop tills with bar code scanners, or cameras designed for small hands. As pupils get older, so Nintendo DS is used in some schools to practice mental arithmetic and PSPs for learning foreign languages.

However, the most widespread changes in recent years in schools are with the technology the teacher uses. Interactive whiteboards are in every school, if not in every class. Many of these are supplemented by add-ons such as wireless keyboards, tablets that can be passed around the room, voting pads and visualisers (a powerful video camera for close up use).

Other personal technologies making headway in schools include MP3 players, to record and play back books or revision notes, and e-readers, such as the Kindle, which are being used for course books as they are easier to cart around – and may be seen as cooler than textbooks, particularly among boys.

Less common in schools, but doubtless on the increase, is the use of more advanced film technologies, such as chroma keying and three-dimensional (3D) filming. The first of these is otherwise known as 'greenscreen' or 'bluescreen' and is the method by which the weather presenter delivers the forecast each morning. A blank screen behind the presenter is filled in electronically with the images being discussed. In schools this could be used to take children to times and places out of their reach, to provide reports and stories.

Although 3D films, and even TV, are on the increase, they are seldom found in schools, although the opportunity has been available for a while – an oversize heart hovering in space, for instance, that can be turned around for everyone to see from all sides, then flown through to follow the route the blood takes. While this is an expensive technology, the price is falling, and 3D cameras to make your own films are beginning to come within the reach of schools.

Schools are also digging into their budgets to fund interactive floor mats, or wall displays, which are triggered by feeds from a CCTV camera. A virtual puddle on the floor ripples as you tread in it, a cymbal on a projected drum kit plays or patches wipe away to reveal another image underneath. These set ups are often accompanied by shafts of light that trigger musical notes, or loops, and even photos or film clips that are thrown onto the wall in response to a child breaking or reflecting the beam back.

These many devices that are entering our schools are changing not only how we work in class, but also what we do. The information we have access to has similarly become more diverse.

Information

Educationalists have been talking for some time about the need to be able to find out, rather than about the need to know. What has been referred to as 'just in time' learning, rather than 'just in case'. The suggestion is that it is no longer sufficient to give children a body of information to carry them through life. Rather, they need to be given the skills to find out what they need to know, when they need to know it. A shift in the curriculum from 'content', – things to know – to 'skills' – the abilities to research, enquire, analyse and communicate.

New technologies are integral to this shift. Often the first instinct when asked a question is to 'google' it – a term that is the name of a product (Google, the most popular search engine on the internet) that has, like 'Hoover', entered the language as a generic term.

One reason for this shift to electronic sources is the speed and ease with which they can be accessed. The challenge in classrooms is to teach children how to evaluate the volume of information they may be presented with and to determine that information's validity.

Apart from speed and choice of sources, finding information online also means it can be presented in different formats. As well as written entries and illustrations, it can be in film, audio or other visual media, such as an animation.

As well as finding information, children can also become creators of it. While they could contribute to Wikipedia as part of their work, they might prefer to borrow the 'wiki' approach and build their own collaborative information source, using a site such as Edublogs. They could also post their animations on YouTube, their podcasts on iTunes and their photos on Flickr. Or maybe they could just add it to the school website, for classmates, parents and relatives to admire and enjoy.

Communication

Sharing our creations through dedicated websites is only one of the ways we now communicate. Where once we relied solely on email and text messaging as alternatives to the phone, now we use multiple channels, and multiple methods within them. Facebook, MySpace and Bebo let us constantly update them with what we are doing to keep friends up to date, and we can upload photos, start campaigns and issue invitations to events using these as well. Twitter encourages us to be short, sharp and to the point, cutting out unnecessary filler, while Skype and MSN, for example, offer voice, video and text contact.

Social networking connects us at many levels, with friends both physical and virtual, and at many ages, with sites such as Club Penguin aimed at pre-teens. (Facebook is intended for those over thirteen years of age.) Virtual professional networks, such as LinkedIn and Plaxo, have sprung up too, along with groups joined by common interests, such as Ravelry for those who enjoy knitting. In addition, for schools sites such as Ning provide secure facilities that can be moderated – that is, an adult can view messages before they are posted – or there are the resources that come with managed learning platforms to connect students within an enclosed, online environment.

Quite often such school resources also provide secure videoconferencing, although video phones and web-enabled handheld devices mean that this is no longer an activity confined to studios with expensive cameras, nor even to computers with cheap webcams. Many schools use text messaging systems to follow up on absences automatically if parents have not phoned in, or to send out blanket messages – perhaps emergency messages announcing an unexpected closure.

Managed learning environments are also offering the potential for more sophisticated channels of communication. As they can be accessed outside of school, through secure log-ins that can be provided for both pupils and parents, it is possible to view information about what is happening in class, as well as looking at up-to-the-minute records of how pupils are doing in school. These include achievement records and attendance data. This is alongside the rather more ordinary use of sending messages and posting information in a similar way to a home/school contact book, only with added video files or photos of the children participating in activities. This kind of contact is especially useful for working with children with more complex special needs.

The same is true for professionals involved with children. They can share information from assessments, notes about recent activities – such as meetings and visits – and even raise concerns, securely and confidentially. The flow of information, the range and the quality, all benefit from those working with a child being able to share what they know simply and quickly.

Create

One of the biggest affects of ICT in recent years has been how it has enabled us to be creative in ways that were previously only within the reach of highly trained professionals with expensive equipment. Film, then video, cameras, for instance, have been widely available for decades; however, now they are cheap and highly portable, our recordings are easily edited and they can be broadcast with a few clicks of a mouse.

The whole process of making a film, of recording, editing, adding titles, giving it a soundtrack, adjusting colour tones and so on, is available through software pre-installed on just about every computer sold, whether Apple or PC.

Technology is enabling us to be creative more easily, and more diversely, than ever before – although simplifying the process does not give any guarantee as to the quality of the outputs. However, it does have an impact in all creative fields. In writing we can still word process, but we can also create blogs or e-books for reading on pocket-sized devices. With audio we can replicate any sound and share our compositions online, as we can with video and photos. We can even create computer games.

Impact on schools

There are many ways in which this diverse range of technologies is making its presence known in our schools, and because of that we need to stay alert to the opportunities that arise and see what we can bring into the classroom to help children learn [STL 8.1 P3,6 and K5,21,30].

Sometimes we may not realise that ICT is being used in a lesson. Electronic keyboards in music, for instance, give children an opportunity to experiment with various sequences as backing tracks, inserting rhythms and switching between loops. All this requires a degree of programming, putting actions in an order and determining the triggers to turn them on and off. Recording the music will mean it can be saved and played back, helping to develop skills around organising files, and mixing it onscreen will mean children are developing creative skills and thinking about engaging with an audience.

In music lessons, then, there are opportunities for 'using ICT to support pupils' learning' [STL 8.1 P1]; to use it in ways that they will find 'stimulating and enjoyable' [STL 8.1 P4]; and to make sure there are a 'range of ICT materials' [STL 8.1 P6]. It is an example of being able to 'integrate ICT into learning activities' [STL 8.2 P2]; to provide 'interesting and stimulating opportunities and challenges' [STL 8.2 P3]; and to help them to use ICT to 'advance their learning' [STL 8.2 P6].

More broadly, when using ICT across the curriculum you will need to know the learning intentions for the subject, and how ICT can help meet these [STL 8 K4,5]. The resources you use could be quite diverse [STL 8 K7], and all benefit the children in different ways [STL 8 K8]. Not only will the pupils be learning about the subject – in this case music – but they will also be developing ICT skills, and you will need to be able to identify these [STL 8 K21] and how you can actively improve them further [STL 8 K22].

ICT in many forms – hardware and software, online and off, mobile and fixed – is now an embedded part of lessons, whether this is the use of probes and sensors in science, video cameras in PE, global positioning systems (GPS) in geography or scientific calculators in maths. Students record what they are doing and demonstrate their learning as text, film, animation, images and sound files. Some of this can be printed, but much of it remains electronic, to be watched on a screen or listened to on an iPod. All of these are activities that are changing the way children, and schools, work. You should be aware of the resources available in school, and how they are booked out, stored and kept safe [STL 7.2 P8,9 and K2,3,25].

Impact on our daily lives

An important aspect of the ICT curriculum is to make sure that children understand its role in our daily lives. We may often be unaware of just how far it has infiltrated: from the technology of the speed camera and CCTV, to the targeted, personalised advertising on Facebook directed at our interests gleaned from the conversations we have, to the self-checkouts at the supermarket – linked to databases to send us offers seeking a greater chunk of our spending – and to the satellites that locate us and guide us to where we want to go.

The technologies we teach children about in school are all around us. The sensors we use to teach about control in class also operate the automatic doors in shops and stop drivers from reversing too far in smart cars. The sequence of steps the robot takes to negotiate the mat on the floor is similar in principle to the programme the washing machine goes through to clean and dry our whites.

Technology has changed the way in which we receive and process information, entertainment, goods and services, and the way we respond to them. It has changed how we connect to each other and the methods and modes of communication; how we can be more than just consumers but also creators of any medium we fancy; and how we participate in society, as citizens and commentators.

Keeping pace [STL 7 K26; STL 8 K30]

With the pace of change as it is, it could seem a daunting task to stay up to date with advances in technology and, in particular, how they impact upon your work and your pupils. In part this should be made easier by the school providing appropriate training as and when necessary. For instance, if a school introduces a learning platform, you would expect to be properly trained to use it. As this will have many of the same functions as social networking websites provide – chat, messaging, forums, wikis, blogs and so on – you will be able to transfer some of the skills you learn to sites that provide these services outside of school (Facebook, Blogger, MSN, etc.) and vice versa.

However, as there are always competing priorities for training time in schools, keeping up to date with ICT is not always top of the list, so you will need to do a lot of this yourself and bring your findings into the classroom. Of course, attending courses outside of school is one possibility, although much professional development is now happening through webinars (online seminars) and web-based courses. You could also visit dedicated shows, such as BETT (the British Educational Training and Technology show).

There is also the press, most of which is available online. The best site for news about ICT and education is www.Agent4change.net, which covers a broad spectrum and includes news, features and interviews. The *Times Educational Supplement* (TES) also has pages dedicated to ICT, both in print and online. Much of this is very practical and focused on classroom practice, although you will have to register, for free, to access some of it.

On the horizon

It is not easy to predict the future, particularly when it comes to new technologies. Many of the changes with the biggest impact have been unforeseen, including the advent of text messaging, Google and Facebook. As memory capacity and battery life develop so will handheld devices. It is perfectly feasible that before 2025 there will be a device capable of recording our every moment from birth until death.

There is also a shift happening from our carrying around all the files and programs we need, to one where we keep everything online and just access them as we need them – so-called 'cloud' computing. We no longer keep our electronic files on our own machines, they are somewhere on the world's network, and when we want to write or edit something we get the application to do it from the web as well.

It is likely that children will all have personal devices in schools in the not too distant future. It is also likely that they will take exams online, potentially sitting them whenever they are ready, rather than at set times.

Many of the possibilities of technology raise moral and ethical issues. Just because we can do something does not mean we have to. Should we, for instance, be able to track everything our children do through their phones, or do they have a right to a private life? All our electronic communications can be recorded, and often are, by the government; if we move to placing all our files and information on the web, should the government also be able to see these. These sorts of questions are also part of the ICT curriculum and will increasingly be raised as technology advances.

Possibly the only certain thing about the technological advances to come is that we will not know about them until they arrive.

5

ICT to communicate

We can use ICT in many ways to connect with others and to get our ideas across. This chapter explores the breadth of these methods, including print media using word processors and desktop publishers; online methods such as email and blogs; and other technologies such as podcasts and videos.

Using word processors

Creating texts of various types has been the most widely used function of a computer in schools. It is a very powerful tool as it allows us to revise and edit until the text says just what we want it to. Other tools mean that everyone is now able to produce professional looking documents; we can alter the appearance in a number of ways so that not just the words but also the presentation appears highly polished.

However, most word processors are designed for literate, adult users who know what they want to say and for whom the in-built tools are a support. For pupils with developing literacy skills these packages may need a bit of tweaking.

The act of writing is fairly complicated, as we do a number of things simultaneously. We decide on the words that will express our thoughts and the order in which they need to go. We spell them selecting the letters that make up the words and, if handwriting, form the letters that make the words by moving the pen accurately across the paper. We also think about the technical elements of grammar, putting the pauses and the emphases in places that give sense to the strings of words. It is not surprising, then, that this task can seem daunting.

With a word processor the task can be staged to make it much more manageable. Pupils can put down words and then read them through afterwards, adding more or reassembling until they get the sense they want, gradually building the structure of the piece. They can spell things pretty much as they want then take time to get the letters in the correct order. Forming the letters properly is done for them by the machine. Punctuation can also be added at the end, perhaps as the child reads it through aloud and gets the sense of where punctuation needs to be. By providing a structure for creating the text in stages, a difficult task becomes much more doable.

Making the word processor pupil-friendly

There are a number of tools built in to computer programs that are designed to be supportive and to make the job easier. Often these do the opposite. You are probably familiar with many of these automatic functions – green and red wavy lines under your text, capital letters that pop into place, words that automatically re-write themselves (type 'adn' and 'and' may take its place). While a useful prop for people whose fingers slip, these can be an off-putting distraction for pupils.

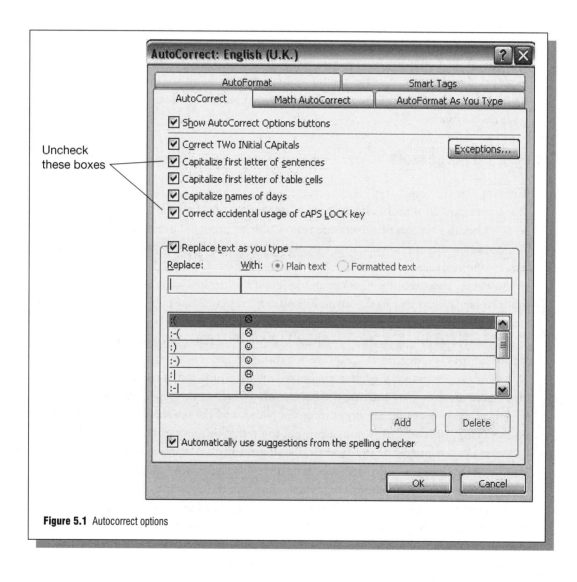

Figure 5.1 Autocorrect options

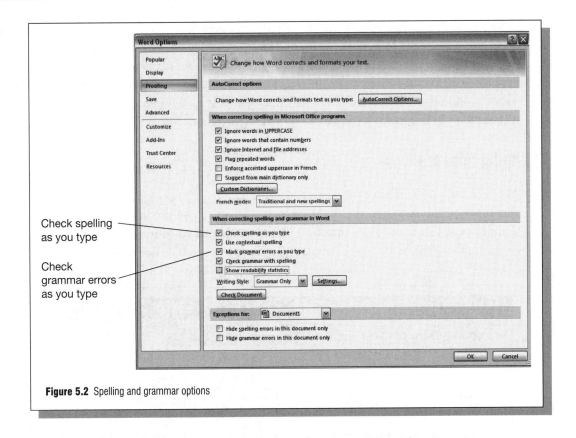

Check spelling as you type

Check grammar errors as you type

Figure 5.2 Spelling and grammar options

The computer may, for example, give each word on a new line a capital letter. This is one of the tools from the Autocorrect menu, along with capitalising the first letter of days of the week. These are not necessarily helpful unless children already know when to use capitals.

To turn these tools off in Microsoft Word (which all schools will have and most use) open **Office Button > Word Options > Proofing > Autocorrect Options** and uncheck the appropriate boxes.

Spellcheckers can be false friends. Apart from decorating the page with wavy red lines, they also do not work with the sense of a sentence but on mathematical principles. The computer compares the set of letters with a database and suggests the nearest grouping rather than the one that makes sense. In some instances, the word is not in the database, such as some peoples' names, in other cases pupils may accept the first word suggested not because it is correct but because of a belief that the computer is smarter than they are when it comes to spelling. Likewise, grammar checkers are not helpful for children working at primary level; they do not take account of the context of what is being written so are not always correct.

To turn off automatic spelling and grammar checking open **Office Button > Word Options > Proofing** and then uncheck 'Check spelling as you type' and 'Check grammar as you type'.

As a general rule it is better to check spellings on a print out than on screen. This means that the pupils will get the text down without distraction, and it allows you to limit the number of words to be checked, to key vocabulary or high frequency words for instance. It will also give opportunities for dictionary work. In fact, it may be preferable to do final editing on a hard copy – a printout – as we sometimes miss on screen what is obvious on paper. To make editing and, indeed, reading easier a couple of other changes to how MS Word is set up are necessary.

Changing appearances

As a general rule text is easier to read if the text size is large and the writing spread out. The font size should be on the order of 14 to 18 points, and the line spacing 1.5 or double. We also need to choose fonts that are easier to read. The majority of fonts use a lower case letter 'A', for instance, that looks similar to an upside down 'G'. For most children this causes

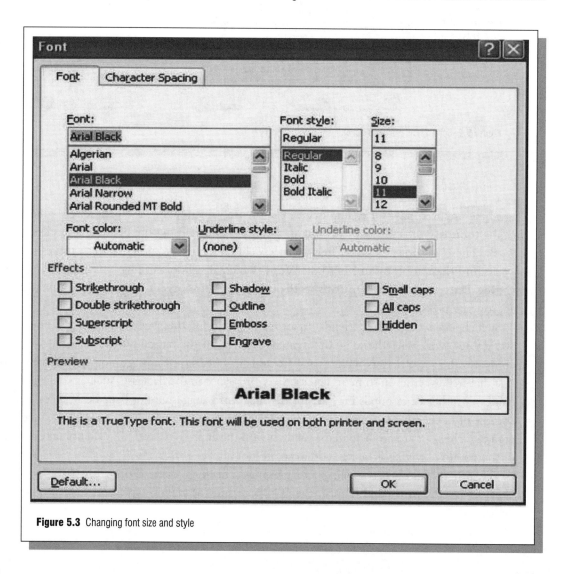

Figure 5.3 Changing font size and style

no problems, but for some it adds to the confusion of decoding. The Comic Sans font has correctly formed letters, as does the Sassoon family of fonts, developed to support young children's development of writing skills. However, some fonts, such as Olde English, can make it hard work for anyone to make sense of the text.

You can change the font style and size for every new document quite easily. Open the **Home** tab and click on the small (arrow) **Font** dialog box button; choose the font and size from the dropdown menus and then click on the **Default** button.

When the dialogue box asks you 'Do you want to change the font to (Default) Comic Sans MS? This will affect all new documents based on the NORMAL Template', click **Yes.**

Changing the line spacing is straightforward; however, permanently changing it is less so as it requires replacing the 'Normal' template. To increase the line spacing open the **Page Layout** tab, then click on the small (arrow) **Paragraph** dialog box button; click on **Line Spacing** and increase it to '1.5 lines' or 'Double', and then click **OK**.

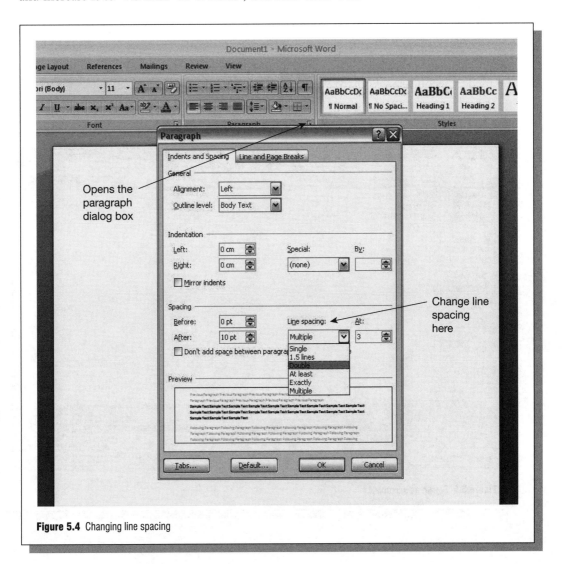

Figure 5.4 Changing line spacing

The word processor as a tool for learning

So far we have looked at how we can use MS Word to structure writing and modify existing tools to make it more useful for our pupils. There are also tools we can create for pupils to use.

A template is a document that remains unchanged in its original format when it is opened and worked on. It allows for many users to start from the same document.

In writing, for instance, it is often helpful to provide pupils with a 'writing frame'. This generally takes the form of a number of sentence starters structured to develop the writing. A piece of instructional writing might be framed as follows:

> You will need
> First you
> Then you
> Next
> After that
> Finally

While this is very simple, it helps children to structure their writing. Writing frames could also be used in secondary school, to write up an investigation perhaps.

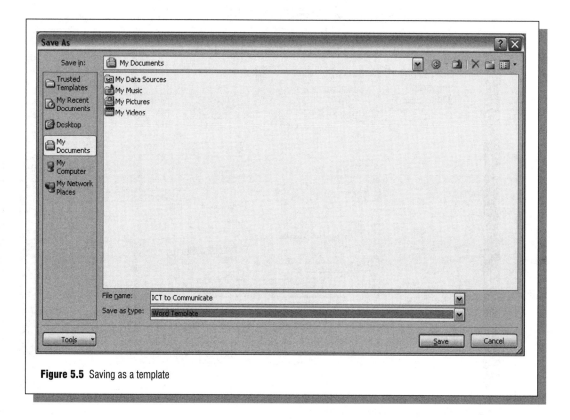

Figure 5.5 Saving as a template

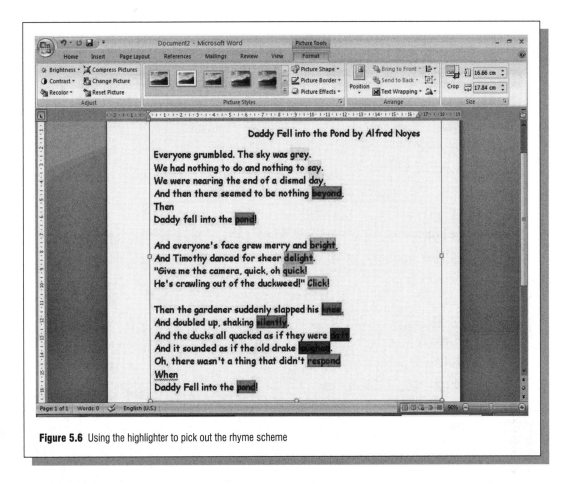

Figure 5.6 Using the highlighter to pick out the rhyme scheme

Creating a template is straightforward, simply:

- type in the structure you want pupils to use
- save it as a template
- close it
- start working on it.

When you have first created your document and are saving it, just change the 'Save as type' box from 'Word Document' to 'Template' and the computer will automatically put it with the other templates that are available.

To use the template simply follow **Office Button > New** then choose the template you created from the list presented.

While we mostly write with a word processor, with a little bit of thought we can make quite creative reading activities too. Above is the poem 'Daddy fell into the pond' by Alfred Noyes. We might want children to focus on the rhyme scheme. Using the Bold, Underline and Italic

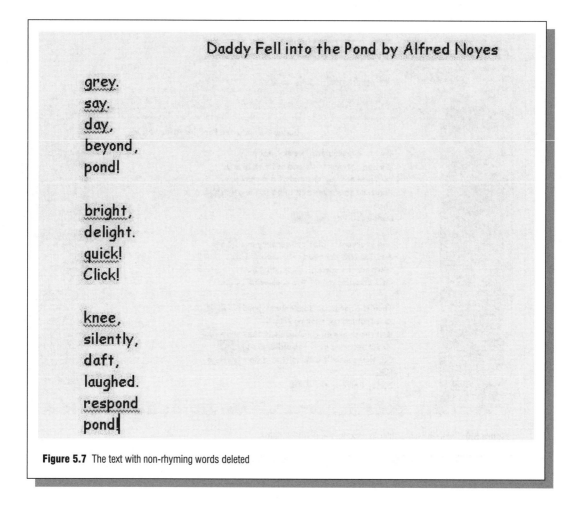

Figure 5.7 The text with non-rhyming words deleted

tools we can ask them to pick it out. Or we could use the **Highlighter** tool to create a multi-coloured version.

Finally, we might just want to look for all the rhyming words. To do this, we might simply delete everything else.

Some rules of word processing

The word processor is a powerful tool, but consideration needs to be given to its use. Here are some thoughts for your guidance:

- Plan before you start writing.
- Write directly onto the computer; do not copy out from a draft book, as this undermines the power of the word processor.

- Do not worry about spelling mistakes until the first draft is written. Turn off distracting spelling and grammar checkers, and do not let pupils use spellcheckers unsupervised.

- Use a simple font with a size of at least 14 points and at least 1.5 line spacing.

- Do the final editing on a hard copy.

- The pupils do not always have to do the typing.

- Exploit the possibilities for collaboration.

Computers can be great motivators that increase concentration and raise self-esteem. They allow all pupils to produce work that at the very least looks professional. As a tool for group work and collaboration they allow several people to work on one piece, either through simply seeing the screen or by sharing work through electronic communication. Computers have endless patience, allowing us to work and rework until we are satisfied.

Using a desktop publisher

Desktop publishing (DTP) packages give you more flexibility when creating documents than word processors. When using the latter, the text starts at the top of the page and moves down as you add more or hit the return key. You can, of course, add images, colour and borders, but the positioning of these are largely governed by the block of writing. With a DTP there is much more flexibility about where everything sits on the page and how it all works together.

Whether creating worksheets to use in lessons or working alongside the pupils to create publications such as newsletters and greetings cards, you will find that a DTP is a powerful tool that will allow you to create work of a professional standard. Increasingly, teaching assistants are supporting children by working outside of the classroom making resources and tailoring them to particular groups or individuals. These programs will enable you to create publications at a professional standard.

Things to remember when using DTP

Because they do not work as other programs do, it is important to remember a few keys points, mainly that you have to select the tool you want to use for the element of the page you are working on, and that when you do, the menus and toolbars will change accordingly. So if you choose the **Text Tool,** the menus and toolbars will become those of a word processor.

Here are a few other things worth remembering (these apply specifically to MS Publisher, but most DTP programs work similarly):

- Everything placed on the page is an 'object', whether it is text, image, table or heading.

- Select the tool to create the type of object you want from the selection offered on the left of the screen.

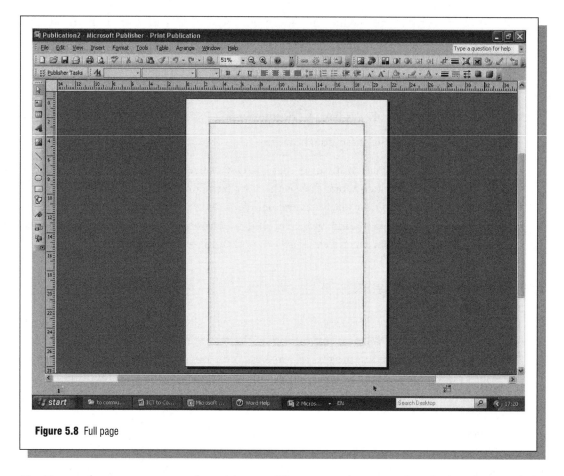

Figure 5.8 Full page

■ Create the area you want that object to fill on your document by placing the crosshairs cursor at one corner, holding down the left mouse button and then pulling to the opposite corner (they are easy to resize, move or delete as you refine your creation).

■ The toolbar and menus at the top of the screen change depending on which type of object you are working with.

■ You will know which object is 'active' because it will have white circles at each corner and on the middle of each side. These are the 'handles' with which you can resize it.

■ To edit an existing object, double click on it. The handles will appear and the menus and toolbars will change.

On this fresh page in MS Publisher, no objects have been created. The **Pointer** tool is chosen and the basic commands are shown at the top. To choose another tool, you simply click on it from the selection on the left and the cursor will change to crosshairs.

Figure 5.9 Crosshairs ready to create a fresh object

The blue lines on the page are just guides, not limits to where you can work. Either ignore them or get rid of them by following **Arrange > Layout guides > Grid guides**.

It is obvious what most of the tools do – the shapes create that shape, the **Table Frame** tool will insert a table, etc. The **Picture Frame** tool offers you the choice of inserting images both from the gallery of graphics provided with the program or from another source, such as digital photos or pictures drawn on the computer, loaded on it or scanned in. Two tools are available to create text, **WordArt** for headings and labels, and **Text Frame** for the 'story'.

When you first start MS Publisher, it offers you a range of formats for documents and different ways to create them.

The opening screen offers you a variety of publications from brochures to menus to websites. If you click on one of these publication options you will then have a choice of design. You can then customise colour schemes and other options such as the number of pages. If you choose **Blank Page Sizes** on the first screen, you are offered a variety of page sizes, from business card size to poster size. Whatever you choose, click on **Create** and you can start.

As you can see from the screenshot below, a number of formats for blank publications are on offer, including cards, banners, posters and web pages.

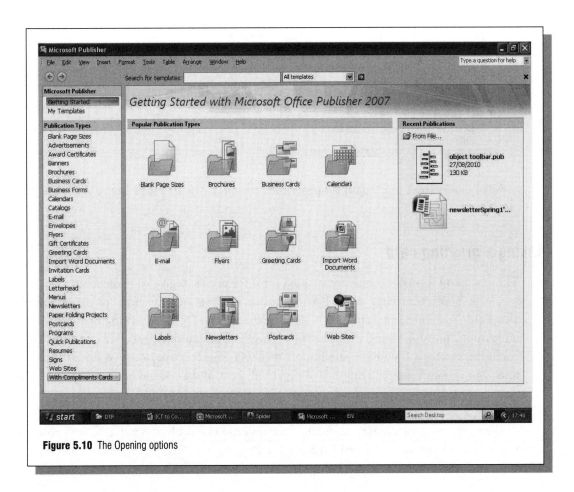

Figure 5.10 The Opening options

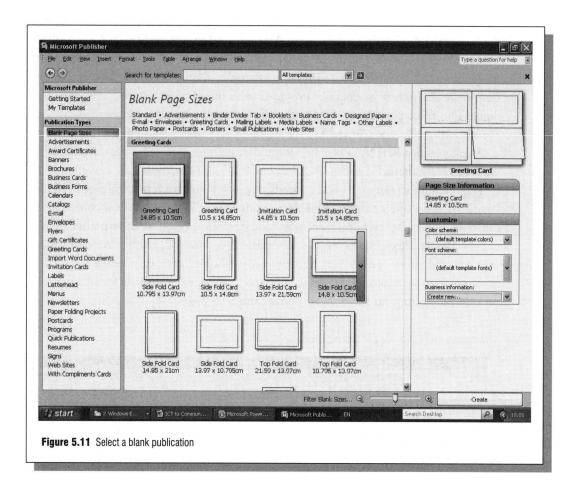

Figure 5.11 Select a blank publication

All of these can be printed on A4 paper then trimmed or glued together to make the finished product.

Making a greeting card

This is a useful format not only for making cards for pupils to give to people, but also to create four page books – or eight pages if you put one inside another. Three formats are available: Side Fold, Top Fold and Tent Fold – all self-explanatory. Double-clicking on anyone of these brings up a prompt asking if you want to insert pages automatically. If you say 'Yes', the computer creates a four-page publication that will print on one sheet of A4 and fold down into your chosen card. The number of pages will be displayed at the bottom of the screen like this: . Clicking on a number will take you to that page.

Creating a greeting card is a useful introduction to DTP for both yourselves and your pupils. It will require you to use **WordArt** for a heading, such as 'Happy Holiday', **Clip Art** for an image on the front, and **Text** for the message on the inside. You may also decide to add coloured backgrounds and borders to any of these.

If you are teaching others, it is best to show them the whole process and then go back and repeat it step by step, with them following you. An interactive whiteboard is ideal for this, but, depending on the size of the group, a large monitor will also do.

Before you start, introduce the task so that they can be thinking of a greeting while you are instructing them. There is usually a suitable event at any time in the year; if Mother's Day, Diwali, Eid or Easter are too far off, there is always, 'Thank you for being my friend' or 'Happy Friday'. Begin by choosing one of the card types and opening it. You will find that the left of the screen is filled by a Format Publication sidebar, which offers page options, colour schemes, font schemes and publication options. Click on the **X** button at the top right of the bar to get rid of this if you do not want to use it.

The first thing to insert is the greeting. Use **WordArt** for this. Click on the [WordArt] button on the tools at the side. The screen will change and a new box will appear for the heading text stating, 'YOUR TEXT HERE'. Replace this with your text. To make the text form a particular shape, click on the dropdown arrow to the left of the toolbar and select one from the options shown. Other tools will allow you to change the font, specifying a particular size, adding shadows and lines or changing the colour of it.

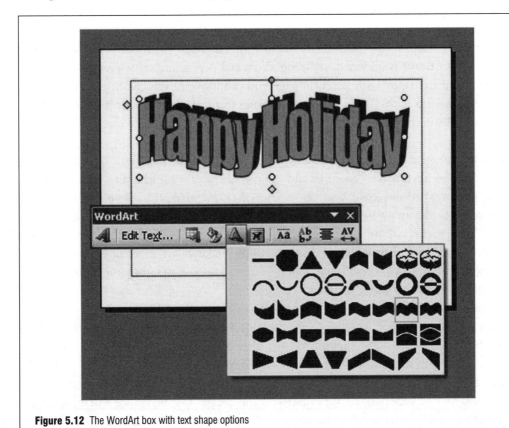

Figure 5.12 The WordArt box with text shape options

If you are happy with your title, click outside of the box to return to the card. The next step is to add an image. This time use the **Picture** tool   .   First you will be asked if you want to choose a picture from clip art or from file or from a scanner or just to create an empty picture frame. Again a dialog box will appear for you to choose the image.

If you select **Clip Art**, a panel on the right gives you a search box into which you type the name of the clip art required. Click **Go**. If you are connected to the internet this might also include the images Microsoft provides on the internet. Once you find the image you want, click on it to select it. It will go onto your page, and you can move it and resize it as you will.

Close the dialog box by clicking on the **X** in the corner to get back to your publication.

You will now have two objects on your page. To move either of them, point at the one you want to move and click on it to make it active and get the handles. As you move the cursor around the page, you will notice it changes to a pair of small, crossed double-ended arrows. If you point at a handle, the cursor becomes a double-ended arrow pointing in the direction in which you can resize the object. If you work on a side, the image will change in one dimension only and can become distorted; if you point at a corner, both height and width will change simultaneously and therefore remain in proportion. Some objects also have another, usually green, dot above them; this is to allow you to rotate the object.

You can place one object on top of the other if you wish, for instance a photo of a bunch of roses as a background and 'Be my Valentine' over the top of it. To do this, simply move one object on top of the other then click on the **Arrange** menu and click on **Order**, then choose either **Send Backward** or **Bring Forward** depending on what you want to happen.

Once you are happy with the front page you can move to the greeting on the inside. Click on the number **3** at the bottom left of the page to move to the right place. For this section you can choose the **Text** tool   . Draw the space in which to write the text. When you begin to type your text, it may be too small to see, in which case you can press the **F9** key at the top of the keyboard to zoom in and again when you are finished to zoom back out.

As with a word processor you can change the font, size and colour before you type, or afterwards. Doing it last has advantages as you can see how any changes will affect the layout, in which case you will need to highlight the text, either by dragging the cursor across all the text or by following **Edit > Select All** or by using the keyboard shortcut **Ctrl + A**. Whichever way you do it, once your text is highlighted you will be able to either use the toolbar or follow **Format > Font** to make the desired changes.

You will also be able to change the background colour and add a plain or patterned border to the box of any object. To change the background colour, simply click on the **Fill** tool, the slightly tipped bucket. By clicking on the dropdown arrow you will have the option of selecting a colour from those shown, clicking on **More Fill Colors** or choosing **Fill Effects**. This last includes gradients, textures, patterns and pictures. It is worth playing with these to get a feel for the variety of backgrounds you can create. Gradients, for instance, are an effect of shading two colours together in different directions across the object.

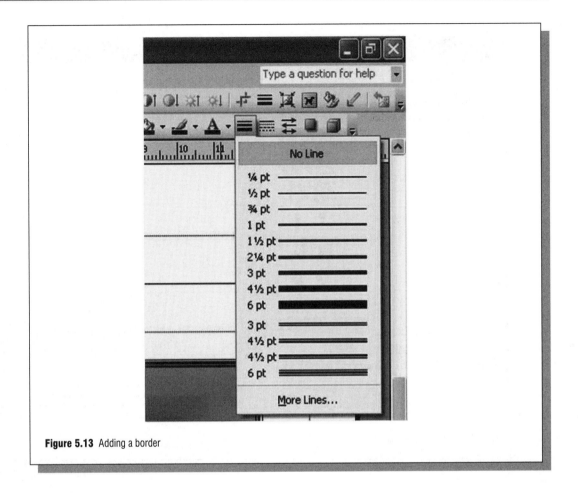

Figure 5.13 Adding a border

To add a border to the object click on the **Line** tool.

This will offer a choice of styles and thicknesses, or you could click on the **Border Art** tab to get a range of effects, including borders made up of images. There is also the option to change the colour and the thickness of the border.

Once you have written the message and changed the font style, size and colour, and then added a background and border, you are ready for the last stage.

Click on the number **4** on the bottom left and the back page will appear. Here you can add another text box showing that it is an original card, designed and printed by you (or the pupils).

Once you have printed it out and looked at it you may decide to make changes. Editing is straightforward. Double click on an object to make it active and change it. Once finished, click away from the object to get rid of the handles and move on to the next alteration.

When using MS Publisher you will find that every so often it prompts you to save your work. This is useful, particularly as these can be large files because of the number of graphics involved.

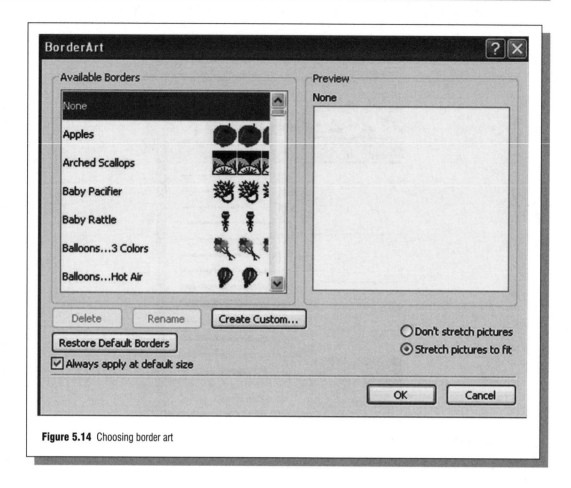

Figure 5.14 Choosing border art

Other publishing packages for pupils

Another simpler desktop publisher for younger children that is very popular in primary schools is 2Publish+ designed for KS1 pupils. It offers a number of templates, such as four-fold cards, wrapping paper and envelopes, and it has very easy to use tools.

To use 2Publish+ choose a template from the opening screen. You may then have the option to choose a simpler or more complicated publication. In the example below (Figure 5.16) you can see a simple leaflet. There is a space for typing and a space for drawing, and the small green arrow at the bottom opens another page of your (six-sided) leaflet. The type, colour and the size of the font can be changed by clicking on the **A** on the top toolbar, and if you have a webcam attached you can capture a picture from the classroom to include in the leaflet. (Click on the webcam button and choose any effects (normal, black and white, sepia, pure monochrome and colourised) you might want and click **OK**; the captured picture will go immediately into the image box. (Click on the spanner icon on the bottom right of the box to choose which webcam to use from the dropdown menu that will appear.)

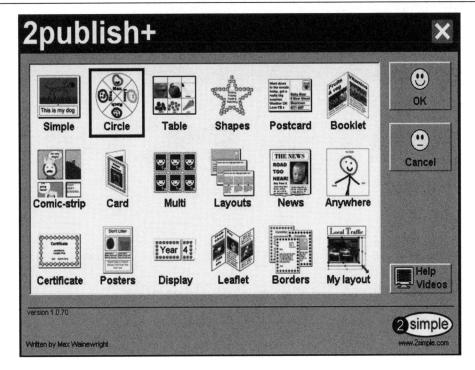

Figure 5.15 2Publish+ templates

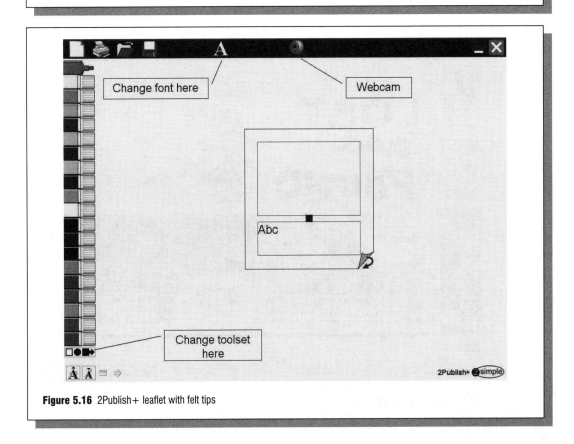

Figure 5.16 2Publish+ leaflet with felt tips

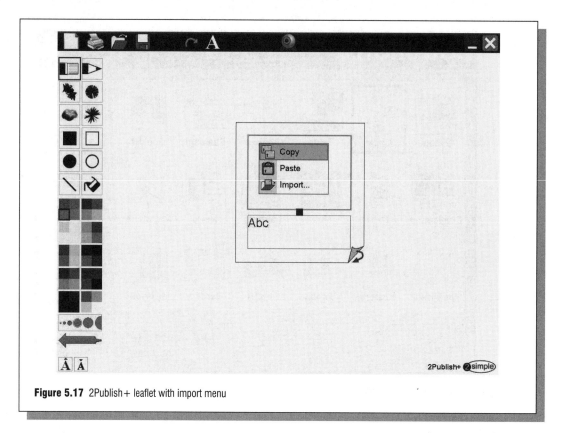

Figure 5.17 2Publish+ leaflet with import menu

Figure 5.18 Making a comic strip with 2Publish+

If you want to use more sophisticated tools, click on the tool selector at the bottom of the felt tip pens. You will then have shape tools, fill tools, spray tools, etc., but when you have chosen this tool set you also have the option to import your own pictures.

Right-clicking on the picture space will give you a dropdown menu that includes **Import**, and from here you can browse to the picture or photograph that you would like to include. To try a simple comic strip, choose a comic strip layout and then click **OK**. In each cell of your strip, you can draw pictures using the felt tips or other drawing tools, import images from your computer or capture images from a webcam. You can then drag speech bubbles from the grey bar on the right of the screen and add text in them to create some dialogue. Drag speech bubbles over the dustbin icon to delete them. You can also add text at the bottom of each cell.

Whatever software you use, desktop publishing lets you and the pupils create exciting, interesting publications, which can be useful regardless of the lesson. They could create: a wanted poster for Goldilocks; an advert for a local history trail; a three-page flyer for or against fox-hunting. The format of the document can help give a context to the learning that makes it more realistic and therefore more effective.

Using graphics packages

A graphic is how we refer to an image generated by a computer, whether it is a drawing, a diagram, a chart or a photo. Some are created from within programs, such as the graphing function in Excel or the drawing tools in Word, but here we are going to look at programs designed for drawing. Drawing is a form of visual expression, and computers can be used for cartooning, doodling, designing and planning and have tools that include pens and ink, brushes, pencils, inked brushes, wax colour crayons, charcoals, chalk, pastels, marker pens and so on.

There are lots of graphics packages available with varying degrees of sophistication. RM Colour Magic, for example, is specifically designed for use in schools and includes functions such as 'stamps' or 'symmetry' and a variety of brushes for, say, oil painting or watercolours. Others, such as PaintShop Photo Pro X3 from Corel or Photoshop CS5 from Adobe, were created with graphic designers and other professionals in mind, so they have advanced features, including allowing painting directly on 3D models, wrapping 2D images around 3D shapes, converting gradient maps to 3D objects, adding depth to layers and text, getting print-quality output and many more.

The basic tools of educational graphics packages are much the same, the differences are generally in the variations available on those tools.

This is a screenshot from probably the most common graphics program, MS Paint. Open Paint by clicking the **Start** button, clicking **All Programs**, clicking **Accessories** and then clicking **Paint**. (This may be different on a networked computer.)

You can use several different tools to draw in Paint. The tool you use and the options you select determine how the line appears in your drawing. You can use pencils, brushes, lines and curve tools. The polygon tool allows you to add your own customised shape as well as being

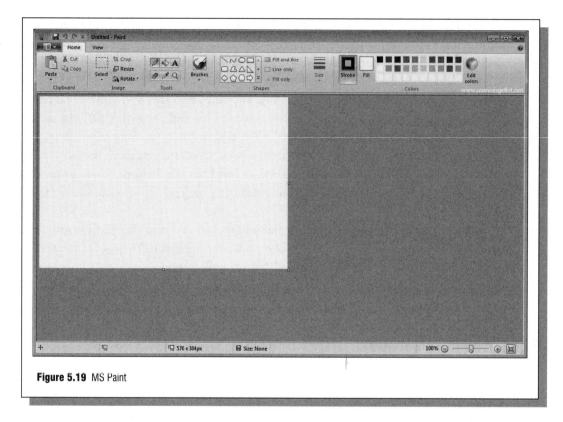

Figure 5.19 MS Paint

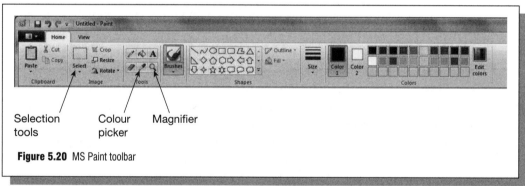

Figure 5.20 MS Paint toolbar

able to add rectangles, ellipses, triangles, arrows, lightning bolts and callouts. And you can add your own text. Most tools are self-explanatory. The **selection** tools are for copying or moving the selected area of the picture to another place. The **magnifier** allows you to work in greater detail, particularly to get rid of the fuzzy edges on drawings. The **colour picker** lets you match a colour on one part of the picture to draw with in another.

The toolbar appears along the top left of the screen, the choice of colours on the top right. The best way to find out how the tools work is to play with them, swapping tools, options for styles and trying out different aspects of the menus.

An exercise that works well with pupils that allows them to try out the tools on any graphics package is to draw an alien. As there is no 'right' answer they can draw quite freely. Using drawing programs is a good way to introduce young children to using the mouse, perhaps drawing a wavy line on screen and asking them to trace it with another colour. Here they have to move the mouse with a button held down. If the program has stamps then these can demonstrate how clicking once can cause something to happen. And using the selection tool can help them learn to 'drag and drop'.

Graphics programs are often used with input devices other than the mouse. A 'graphics tablet' is a pad rather like a mouse mat, with a special pen attached. As the user 'draws' on the pad so the image appears on screen, much more similar to real drawing than using a mouse.

Many classrooms now have interactive whiteboards or touch screen monitors. These allow you to use your finger (or a special pen) instead of the mouse. For young children and those with special educational needs, this immediacy is a good introduction to computer use. Simple exercises, such as writing or tracing their name on screen, can help to develop fine motor control and handwriting skills.

Graphics tools can be used to explore other subjects too. Here perspective is explored using 2Paint a Picture.

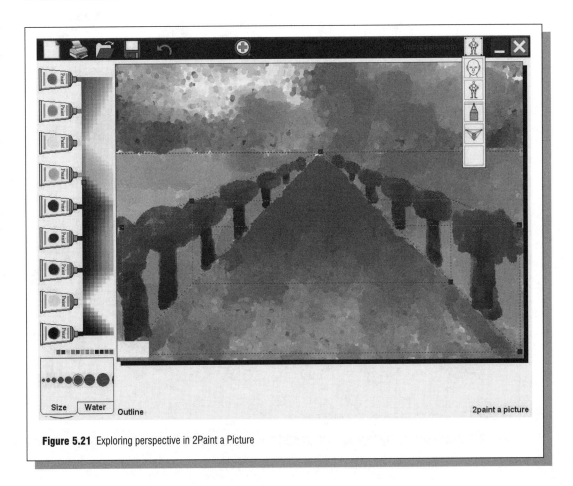

Figure 5.21 Exploring perspective in 2Paint a Picture

Or the stamps can be used for counting exercises. Here a number of toys have been stamped to make rows of five using the stamps from the library in Colour Magic. With older pupils the shape stamps can be used to explore patterns and tessellations.

Throughout the ICT curriculum, pupils are required to combine text and graphics. In the early stages this could be adding a caption to a drawing. Later on it may be creating a treasure map and pasting it into Word or creating their own illustrations for a story in PowerPoint.

Animating your drawings and cartoons is another activity that is easy to do with the right software. 2Animate is a program that works like a zoetrope or like little flip books. You draw your cartoons several times with small changes in each drawing and when watched one after the other at speed it looks like your figures are moving. The resulting animated GIF (graphics interchange format) file can be inserted into a PowerPoint presentation or into 2Create a Story (as noted in Chapter 7) or published onto a webpage. As well as drawing you can capture (from a digital camera or webcam) or scan images into your sequence of pictures, then click on play and watch your animation. 2Animate has differentiated user levels and can be used

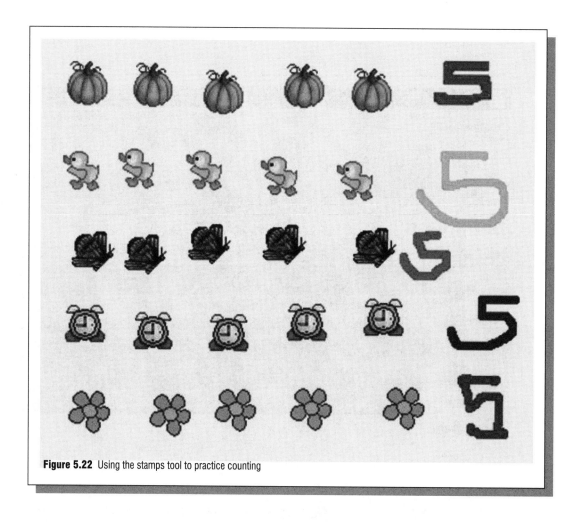

Figure 5.22 Using the stamps tool to practice counting

Figure 5.23 2Animate screen

across the curriculum, for example: to show gravity, how a seed grows or how a caterpillar becomes a butterfly.

As with any application, adding a graphic can be done in several ways. If the drawing program is open, it can generally be copied from the File menu then pasted, again from the same menu. Or it must be saved in the program that created it and then can be added through the Insert menu, following **Insert > Picture > From File** then browsing to find the image.

Using computer graphics can be quite stimulating for pupils as the results can often be more sophisticated than they can achieve using conventional means such as paper and paint. They also allow pupils to add colour and explanation to written texts in ways that would be more difficult without the computer.

Communicating online

Most of us use email and, of course, children need to learn how to use it, though many of them already use it at home. In early KS2 children might start by learning that you can send comments to a website using an online form – say their local newspaper, or CBBC – and they can discuss the advantages or disadvantages of doing so. They could also use a web discussion, perhaps on a blog or on the school's managed learning environment (MLE; see Chapter 9), to contribute to a class topic or get feedback from teachers and fellow pupils. Some MLEs provide visual email tools that allow younger children to send messages to their classmates by simply clicking on their friend's picture, from a list of classmates to which they have access. They can then write a message, draw a picture or record a sound to send to their friend.

At upper KS2, students should be able to send and receive attachments with email and open files from their online web space (the MLE); they should be able to use address books, the CC and BCC fields and folders.

A project that uses email to bring together classes in schools in different parts of the country (say one rural and one urban) is a good way of doing all this – even better if the two schools are in different countries. It will, at the same time, cover other areas of the curriculum – for instance, geography, where children have to compare contrasting localities. Once the link has been established between the teachers of classes in the two schools, the children can be paired up with their 'email pen friends'. As well as swapping personal details, the children can be directed to ask questions about the locality of the other school and can answer questions about their own locality and send photos as attachments.

It is always a good idea to give children opportunities to communicate in different ways. Some are much more comfortable and open when writing than speaking and some the other way round. Using online discussions and forums can be the ideal way for some children to communicate, but it should be impressed on children that web discussions differ from email in that they are more public and so more people will see contributions.

Using podcasts to communicate

You can read about how to make a podcast – such as a radio broadcast on the internet – in Chapter 8, but how useful they are can be seen in the following example.

A group of a dozen children were chosen because of their difficulties with writing. A whole range of skills is required for making a podcast: imagination, creativity, collaboration; speaking and listening; reading and writing; and ICT. The children paired up, had their discussions and then wrote scripts for their items. One pair wrote jokes and riddles, another pair decided to interview people in school about their favourite games, two wanted to do a news article and a quiz about football and two wanted to record a news report about Sir Francis Drake. They recorded their work on MP3 recorders, edited their recordings using Audacity and posted them on the school website for their parents and friends to enjoy. In fact, it gave them a potential audience of thousands for their work. Podcasts can be interactive; the audience can be invited to send in their comments, giving valuable feedback to the children about their work.

6

Working with data

Gathering and analysing information is one of the key roles of technology. This chapter explores how this is done in the classroom: how we gather information and the ways in which we can understand and interpret it. This includes determining which information can be trusted. It also includes using data logging equipment and sensors to gather information that can then trigger something else to happen, and the programming of that sequence.

Using spreadsheets

Although we mainly use our machines for creating written documents, their original purpose, as the name 'computer' suggests, was for calculating, for handling bits of data. It is with spreadsheets and databases that we do this on modern desktops.

Essentially a spreadsheet is a large table made up of columns and rows into which we put the words and figures we want to work with, called data. Data needs a context in order to give it meaning, for instance '26' might be a house number, the temperature outside, the number of people in a lottery syndicate or the goals conceded by Charlton Athletic at home last week. Spreadsheets can be used to perform calculations and to keep records. This latter use means making the spreadsheet work as a database, a way of sorting and ordering the information – in date or alphabetical order perhaps – in order to answer questions. Many schools keep track of children's progress on a spreadsheet such as Figure 6.1 overleaf.

There are times when you will be harnessing the power of the spreadsheet to do both, to do calculations and to sort the answers. In your own work you might use a writing tracker to record a child's progress through certain targets and then follow the rate at which these are being achieved (see Figure 6.2).

With children you might gather weather information from around the world, then work out average temperatures and rainfall and compare places as holiday destinations.

The most widely used spreadsheet is Microsoft Excel. Here several pages, or worksheets, can be used simultaneously and information from one page can be used to do calculations or

Forename	Surname	Gend	Born	KS1 SATs			Summer Year 3			Summer Year 4			Summer Year 5	
				Readi	Writi	Matl	Readi	Writi	Mat	Readi	Writi	Math	Readi	Writi
Abdul	Hilal	M	08/07/98										4c	3b
Ahmed	Sheuli	M	08/01/98	2c	2c	2b	2b	2a	2a	3b	3b	3b	4c	3a
Ahmed	Sheema	F	20/05/98	2a	2a	2b	3a	2a	2b	4c	4c	3c	4a	4b
Ahmed	Shazia	M	12/02/98	2a	2b	2a	3c	3c	2b	4c	3a	3c	4b	4c
Akthar	Shajibur	F	28/11/97	2b	2b	2c	2b	3c	2b	4c	3a	2a	4c	4c
Akther Tannie	Samirah	F	09/12/97	3	3	2a	3a	3c	3c	4b	4c	3a	5c	4a
Al-Hassan	Sadia	M	09/06/98	2b	2c	2b	2a	3c	2a	3b	3b	3b	3a	3a
Alom	Sabnam	M	17/03/98	2c	2c	2c	2b	2b	2a	2a	3c	3c	3a	3b
Amin Ahmed	Riyaadh	M	17/10/97	2a	2a	3	3a	3c	3b	4b	3a	3a	4a	4b
Begum	Rabbia	F	07/03/98	2a	2a	2a	3b	3a	3c	4c	4c	3b	4a	4b
Begum	Nusrat Rehena	F	16/12/97	3	2a	3	3c	3c	3c	4b	4c	3a	4a	4b
Begum	Nasim	F	30/10/98							4c	3b	3c	4a	4b
Begum Hussain	Muhin	F	28/12/97	2b	2b	2b	3c	2a	3c	4c	3b	3b	4b	4c
Cheeseman	Md.Ruhul	F	29/05/98	2b	2c	2c	2b	2c	2b	2b	3c	2a	3a	3a
Haydar	Md Kahar	M	28/04/98	1	1	1	1b	1a	2b	2c	2b	1a	2a	2a
Hussain Syed	Mazeda	M	20/08/98	3	3	3	3c	3c	3c	4c	4c	3b	4a	4b
Islam	Masum	F	05/09/97	2b	2b	2b	2a	2b	2c	3c	3b	3b	4c	3a
Izzet	Sandra	F	29/07/98	3	3	3	3a	3c	2a	4b	4c	3b	4a	4b
Khan	Kaief	M	04/08/98	2a	2a	2a	3a	3c	2a	4b	3a	3b	4a	4b
Khatun	Kaazim	F	24/03/98				P	P	w	p4	p5	p5	p6	p6
Md.Abdalla	Farzana	M	18/10/97	1	1	2b	1b	2c	3c	2b	2b	2a	3c	3c
Miah	Hasan	M	16/05/98	2b	2b	2a	2b	2a	2a	3c	3b	3b	3b	3a
Rahman	Halima	M	19/04/98	2c	2c	1	2c	2c	2a	2b	2b	1a	3c	2a

Figure 6.1 Pupil tracker illustration

create charts and graphs on another. On a spreadsheet, each column has a letter as a heading, and each row a number; this means that each individual cell has its own address, or reference, such as A4 or FJ65.

Using a spreadsheet for record keeping

Creating a table is very straightforward. Simply start a new worksheet then type the data into an empty cell, click in another one and add some more. To move quickly between cells either press the **Tab** key to move to the right or the **Return** or **Enter** key to move down. You will probably want to give your columns, and maybe your rows, titles or headings to describe the data. It is important not to leave blank rows because this prevents some tools from working fully.

Figure 6.3 is an extract from a spreadsheet used as a database by a SEN coordinator (SENCO) to keep track of pupils with special educational needs in the school.

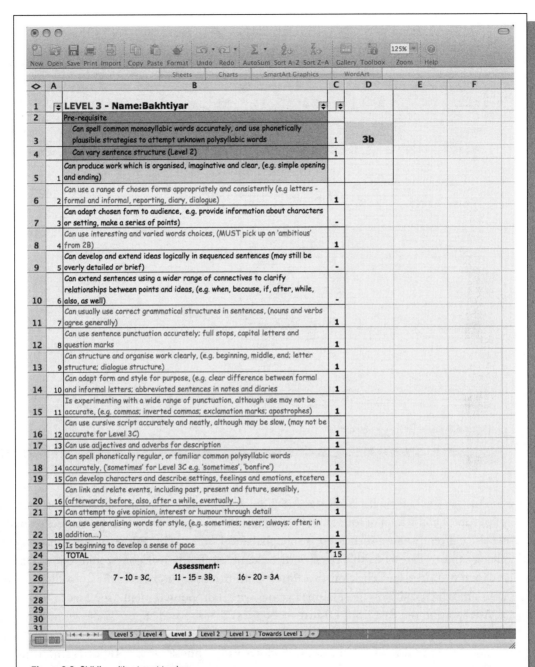

Figure 6.2 Child's writing target tracker

	A	B	C	D	E	F	G	H	I
1					**SEN**	Communication	cognition and	behaviour, emotional	sensory or
2	Surname	Forename	Gender	Born	stage	and language	learning	and social development	physical difficulties
3	Abdalla	Naima	F	08/10/98	School action plus			1	
4	Ahmed	Ruheth	M	19/03/99	School action plus			1	
5	Aiysha	Siddiqa	F	14/05/99	School action			2	
6	Akthar	Yassin Esha	F	09/04/99	School action plus				
7	Amin	Aminoor	M	05/08/99	School action plus	2			1
8	Begum	Arfa	F	17/11/98	School action		1		1
9	Begum	Danny	F	03/05/00	statement		1		
10	Chaiwalla	Fahmida	F	12/04/01	School action	1		1	
11	Chowdhury	Farzana	F	17/09/98	School action plus		1		1
12	Chowdhury	Jihad	F	21/10/01	School action plus			1	
13	Ferdous	Mahima	F	01/05/99	statement			1	
14	Haydar	Maksood	M	08/08/00	School action plus	1			
15	Hoque Amin	Md. Asad	M	05/12/03	School action			2	
16	Hussain	Rizwa Nur	F	19/03/05	School action	1			
17	Hussain	Md. Ruhul	F	27/09/98	School action		2		
18	Islam	Mohsin	F	21/08/06	School action	1			
19	Ismail	Naim	M	15/11/98	School action plus	1			
20	Ismat	Sadia	F	27/07/02	School action plus				1
21	Kamali	Samirah	M	25/10/98	School action		1		
22	Khan	Samiya Selina	M	29/08/02	School action plus			1	
23	Khan	Shah Ifthikhar	M	05/01/99	statement				1
24	Khan	Shah Md. Abu	M	08/02/99	School action plus			1	
25	Khatun	Shahan	F	21/05/99	statement		1		
26	Rahman	Taher	M	07/01/07	statement	1			1
27	Rahman	Tahsin	M	22/04/99	School action				1

Figure 6.3 An extract from a SEN register

The data includes what SEN stage (School Action, School Action Plus or Statement) the pupils are at and which of four categories represents their primary, and in some cases secondary, needs. Currently the information is in alphabetical order. The **Filter** facility can be used to change this to date of birth ('Born' in the example). To do this you would follow **Data** tab > **Sort & Filter** and click on the **Filter** button. This switches on the auto filter for each column, which will now have a small arrow with a dropdown menu (see Figure 6.4).

After sorting the data from **Oldest to Newest** the data will appear as shown in Figure 6.5. The oldest children come first because the data is in ascending order.

The **Filter** facility of the spreadsheet allows us to choose which **Records** (individual sets of data) we want to see. For instance, I may only want to see pupils with statements (see Figures 6.6 and 6.7).

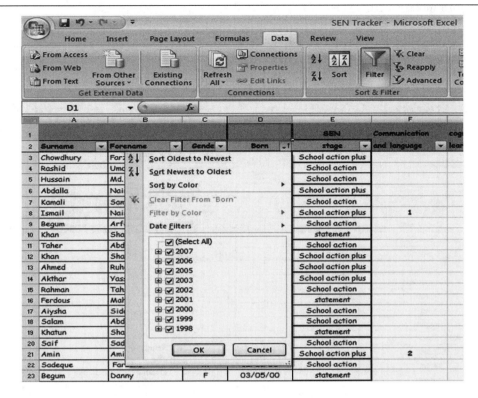

Figure 6.4 Sort & Filter dropdown menu

Surname	Forename	Gende	Born	SEN stage	Communication and language	cognition and learning	behaviour, emotional and social developme	sensory or physical difficult
Chowdhury	Farzana	F	17/09/98	School action plus		1		1
Rashid	Umara	M	17/09/98	School action				
Hussain	Md. Ruhul	F	27/09/98	School action		2		
Abdalla	Naima	F	08/10/98	School action plus			1	
Kamali	Samirah	M	25/10/98	School action		1		
Ismail	Naim	M	15/11/98	School action plus	1			
Begum	Arfa	F	17/11/98	School action		1		1
Khan	Shah Ifthikhar	M	05/01/99	statement				1
Taher	Abdul	M	08/01/99	School action				
Khan	Shah Md. Abu	M	08/02/99	School action plus			1	
Ahmed	Ruheth	M	19/03/99	School action plus			1	
Akthar	Yassin Esha	F	09/04/99	School action plus				1
Rahman	Tahsin	M	22/04/99	School action				1
Ferdous	Mahima	F	01/05/99	statement			1	
Aiysha	Siddiqa	F	14/05/99	School action			2	
Salam	Abdul	M	17/05/99	School action				
Khatun	Shahan	F	21/05/99	statement		1		
Saif	Sadia	F	03/06/99	School action				
Amin	Aminoor	M	05/08/99	School action plus	2			1
Sadeque	Farzana	M	12/01/00	School action				
Begum	Danny	F	03/05/00	statement		1		
Haydar	Maksood	M	08/08/00	School action plus	1			
Chaiwalla	Fahmida	F	12/04/01	School action	1		1	
Chowdhury	Jihad	F	21/10/01	School action plus			1	
Ismat	Sadia	F	27/07/02	School action plus				1

Figure 6.5 SEN register in date-of-birth order

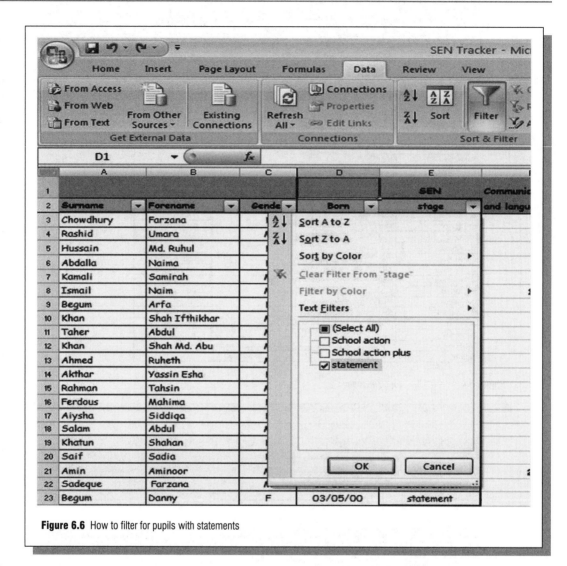

Figure 6.6 How to filter for pupils with statements

	Surname	Forename	Gend	Born	SEN stage	Communication and language	Cognition and learning	Behaviour, emotional and social developr	Sensory or physical difficulty	
3	Khan	Ifthakur	m	05/01/1999	statement					1
4	Ferdous	Mahima	f	01/05/1999	statement			1		
5	Khatun	Shahana	f	21/05/1999	statement		1			
6	Smith	Danni	f	03/10/2000	statement		1			
7	Rahman	Taher	m	07/01/2001	statement	1				1

Figure 6.7 Pupils with statements

Or just the girls (see Figure 6.8):

	A Surname	B Forename	C Gender	E SEN stage	F Communication and language	G cognition and learning	H behaviour, emotional and social developme	I sensory or physical difficult
3	Chowdhury	Farzana	F	School action plus		1		1
5	Hussain	Ruhula	F	School action		2		
6	Abdalla	Naima	F	School action plus			1	
9	Begum	Arfa	F	School action		1		1
14	Akthar	Yassin Esha	F	School action plus				
16	Ferdous	Mahima	F	statement			1	
17	Aiysha	Siddiqa	F	School action			2	
19	Khatun	Shahana	F	statement		1		
20	Saif	Sadia	F	School action				
23	Begum	Danni	F	statement		1		
25	Chaiwalla	Fahmida	F	School action	1		1	
26	Chowdhury	Jane	F	School action plus			1	
27	Ismat	Sadia	F	School action plus				1
30	Hussain	Razia	F	School action	1			
31	Islam	Masuma	F	School action	1			

Figure 6.8 Spreadsheet filtered for girls

Or only those with communication and interaction difficulties (see Figure 6.9):

	A Surname	B Forename	C Gender	E SEN stage	F Communication and language	G cognition and learning	H behaviour, emotional and social developme	I sensory or physical difficult
8	Ismail	Naim	M	School action plus	1			
21	Amin	Aminoor	M	School action plus	2			1
24	Haydar	Maksood	M	School action plus	1			
25	Chaiwalla	Fahmida	F	School action	1		1	
30	Hussain	Razia	F	School action	1			
31	Islam	Masuma	F	School action	1			
32	Rahman	Taher	M	statement	1			1

Figure 6.9 Filtered for communication difficulties

Or even only those children who meet two of these criteria, say, girls with communication difficulties (see Figure 6.10):

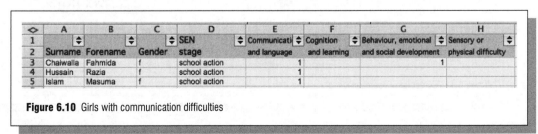

	A Surname	B Forename	C Gender	D SEN stage	E Communicati and language	F Cognition and learning	G Behaviour, emotional and social development	H Sensory or physical difficulty
3	Chaiwalla	Fahmida	f	school action	1		1	
4	Hussain	Razia	f	school action	1			
5	Islam	Masuma	f	school action	1			

Figure 6.10 Girls with communication difficulties

The **Filter** function lets you narrow the records down to see only those that meet specific criteria. To stop filtering by that criteria simply click on **Select All**.

Databases in the curriculum

The **Sort** and **Filter** functions allow us to interrogate data, to ask questions of it. Spreadsheets such as Excel are just one of the tools used to handle data in lessons. Other programs are specifically designed for the purpose and therefore can be easier to use as they offer more support to the user. Essentially though, they are doing the same thing, allowing users to ask questions of data.

The following spreadsheet on pets can be interrogated by skin type, classification or number of legs (see Figure 6.11).

With a database designed for school children you might get a search screen like this that uses a number of questions to perform the filtering function (see Figure 6.12).

Here you can see the term, 'Type the same as Mammal', has already been selected and 'Or number of legs equal to 4' is about to be added. This will show all mammals or any other animals that have four legs.

	A	B	C	D	E
1	Animal	Name	Skin type	Number of legs	Classification
2	Rat	Ratty	Fur	4	Mammal
3	Rabbit	Floppy	Fur	4	Mammal
4	Parrot	Mr Big	Feathers	2	Bird
5	Guinea Pig	Snuffles	Fur	4	Mammal
6	Goldfish	Goldie	Scales	0	Fish
7	Snake	Sid	Skin	0	Reptile
8	Horse	Fleetfoot	Fur	4	Mammal
9	Budgie	Swoop	Feathers	2	Bird
10	Dog	Nelson	Fur	4	Mammal
11	Cat	Tibbles	Fur	4	Mammal
12	Cat	Blackie	Fur	4	Mammal
13	Mouse	Squeak	Fur	4	Mammal
14	Terrapin	Speedy	Skin	4	Reptile

Figure 6.11 Extract from a spreadsheet about pets

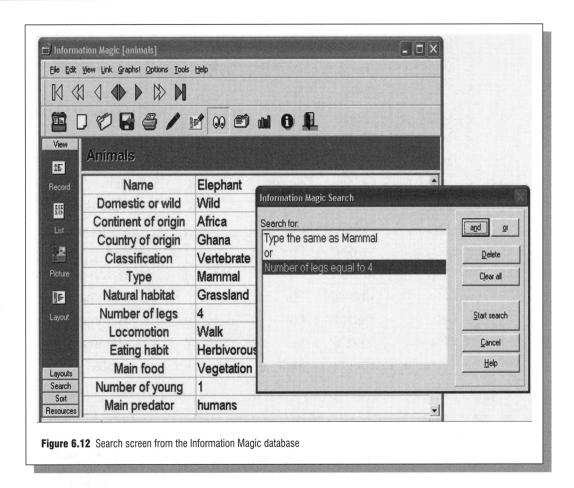

Figure 6.12 Search screen from the Information Magic database

Creating a graph

All data handling programs will create charts and graphs from the information you provide. In Excel this is done by highlighting the cells to be included, then clicking on the **Insert** tab and, from the **Charts** menu, choosing the kind of chart you want from the many available.

Select cells, rows or columns that are not adjacent by holding down the **Control** key while selecting.

To create a bar chart showing how many legs each animal has, you would start by highlighting the 'Animal' and the 'Number of legs' columns (see Figure 6.13).

Clicking on the **Insert** tab and the tiny button in the corner of the Charts section gives you a dropdown menu that allows you to choose the type of chart required (see Figure 6.14).

To complete the chart, click **Next**, adding labels and a title as you go. When you click **Finish**, your chart will appear (see Figure 6.15).

	A	B	C	D	E
1	Animal	Name	Skin type	Number of legs	Classification
2	Rat	Ratty	Fur	4	Mammal
3	Rabbit	Floppy	Fur	4	Mammal
4	Parrot	Mr Big	Feathers	2	Bird
5	Guinea Pig	Snuffles	Fur	4	Mammal
6	Goldfish	Goldie	Scales	0	Fish
7	Snake	Sid	Skin	0	Reptile
8	Horse	Fleetfoot	Fur	4	Mammal
9	Budgie	Swoop	Feathers	2	Bird
10	Dog	Nelson	Fur	4	Mammal
11	Cat	Tibbles	Fur	4	Mammal
12	Cat	Blackie	Fur	4	Mammal
13	Mouse	Squeak	Fur	4	Mammal
14	Terrapin	Speedy	Skin	4	Reptile

Figure 6.13 Highlighting non-adjacent columns to create a chart

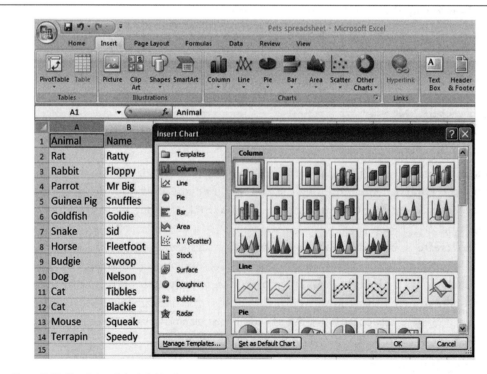

Figure 6.14 The choice of charts in Excel

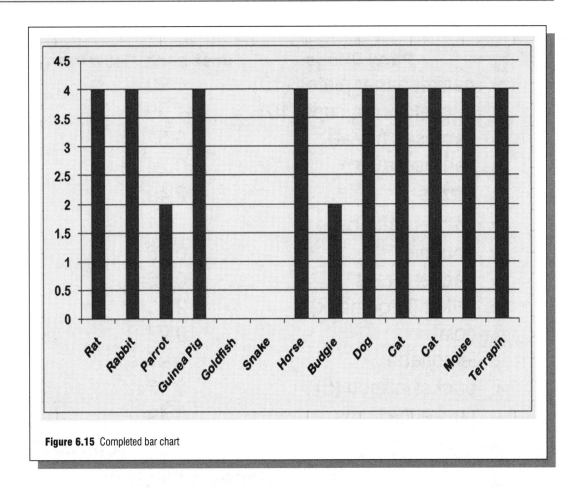

Figure 6.15 Completed bar chart

Using a spreadsheet to do calculations

One of the most useful functions of a spreadsheet is to do calculations instantly, and recalculate, much faster than can be done using pencil and paper or a calculator.

When using a spreadsheet to do calculations there are a couple of things it is important to remember: first, that formulae always start with an equals sign '='; second, that while plus and minus remain '+' and '-' (though note that Excel uses a hyphen for the minus sign), divide becomes '/' and times '*'.

A typical activity with pupils (or even for your own purposes) is to use the spreadsheet to calculate the cost of holding a party. In this example, there are a restricted number of food and drink items and the prices are given, as below (see Figure 6.16).

The cost currently does not have a pound sign, but we can add this automatically. First of all the whole column is highlighted by clicking on its letter, B in this case. Then choose the Home tab and from the Number menu click the dropdown menu (which has General written inside it and choose Currency (see Figure 6.17).

	A	B	C
1	**Party things**	**cost each**	**How many?**
2	packet paper plates (10)	1.99	
3	packet plastic cups (10)	1.99	
4	samosas (meat)	0.55	
5	samosas (veg)	0.24	
6	pizzas	2.49	
7	packet Jaffa cakes	0.1	
8	doughnut	0.16	
9	packet crisps	0.46	
10	Kitkat (large pack)	2.38	
11	cola	0.97	
12	lemonade	0.97	
13	packet lollipop (5)	2.13	
14	packet balloons	0.49	
15			**Total cost:**
16		**Money collected:**	
17		**Left to spend:**	
18			

Figure 6.16 Calculating the costs of a party

Now when data is entered it will automatically be set out as pounds and pence. The same formatting can be applied to row D.

You can see from the list the various types of data format that can be used. This can help make sure that particular columns conform to particular types of data, such as dates or percentages. However, any entry that mixes letters and numbers – postcodes for instance – can only be in the **Text** format.

To calculate the amount spent on each item we will multiply the 'Number of items' by the cost per item, so if we wanted 3 packs of paper plates we would multiply 3 by £1.99.

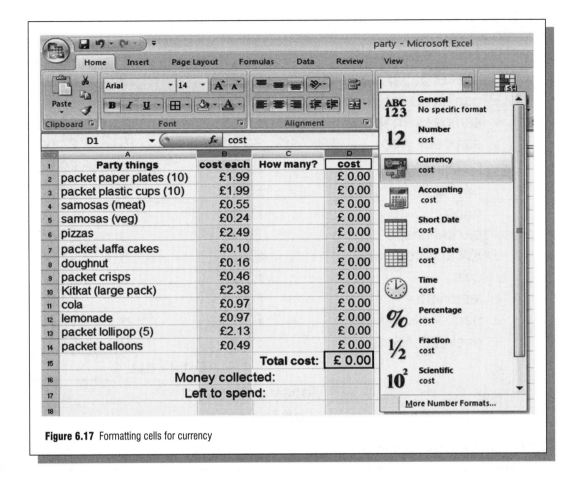

Figure 6.17 Formatting cells for currency

The point of using a spreadsheet is that it lets us try different numbers and will, if we set it up properly, recalculate automatically each time. When we use a formula, we can tell the computer to multiply the contents of one cell by the contents of another, in this case cell C12 (the number of bottles of lemonade) by cell B12 (the price per bottle); if either number is changed the 'Cost' column will change automatically. The formula in cell D2 will be =B2*C2, and the one in D3 will be =B3*C3 and so on down.

Into cell D2 enter = and click on **cell B2**, then enter * and click on **cell C2**. The formula will be entered into the cell and, to copy the formulas quickly into lower rows, we can pick up the small black handle on the corner of the cell and pull it down over the rest of the cells beneath.

Now when we start our shopping list the amount we are spending will be automatically filled in, as shown in Figure 6.18.

Finally, we need to know how much the 'Total Cost' is and take it away from the money collected to see how much we have left to spend. We want to know the **SUM** spent. Again we are not going to put in each individual amount, =£6.90+£7.50+£7.00 and so on; instead

	A	B	C	D
1	**Party things**	**cost each**	**How many?**	**cost**
2	packet paper plates (10)	£1.99	3	£5.97
3	packet plastic cups (10)	£1.99	3	£5.97
4	samosas (meat)	£0.55	15	£8.25
5	samosas (veg)	£0.24	15	£3.60
6	pizzas	£2.49	4	£9.96
7	packet Jaffa cakes	£0.10	5	£0.50
8	doughnut	£0.16	20	£3.20
9	packet crisps	£0.46	10	£4.60
10	Kitkat (large pack)	£2.38	5	£11.90
11	cola	£0.97	5	£4.85
12	lemonade	£0.97	5	£4.85
13	packet lollipop (5)	£2.13	6	£12.78
14	packet balloons	£0.49	2	£0.98
15			**Total cost:**	
16		**Money collected:**		
17		**Left to spend:**		

Figure 6.18 Party with costs filled in

we are going to tell the computer which cells to add up. It would be laborious if we had to put in each one, so we just use the range of cells by specifying the first one and the last one with a colon between and put this in brackets. In this case, that is (D2:D14). As always the formula begins with an '=' sign, and we are using the sum function, so it comes out as '=SUM(D2:D14)'. If you get any part of it wrong the computer will flag it up with '#Value' or '#NAME?' to let you know that something is amiss.

If we assume there are thirty children in the class, each bringing in £3.00 for the party, this will give us £90.00 'Money collected'. The amount 'Left to spend' will then be =90-D15, because this value (£90) is not going to change. The formulas in your final spreadsheet are shown in Figure 6.19.

When used in this way a spreadsheet can be thought of as a 'model'; that is, a representation of a real situation that we can use to ask, 'What if?' questions. 'What if we get another packet of samosas?' or 'What if the price of pizzas goes up, how many can we afford then?' The idea in this simulation is to spend all the money, and it is important for the adults working with the children to help them focus on the real situation. They could buy 20 pizzas and 20 bottles

	A	B	C	D
1	**Party things**	**cost each**	**How many?**	**cost**
2	packet paper plates (10)	1.99	3	=B2*C2
3	packet plastic cups (10)	1.99	3	=B3*C3
4	samosas (meat)	0.55	15	=B4*C4
5	samosas (veg)	0.24	15	=B5*C5
6	pizzas	2.49	4	=B6*C6
7	packet Jaffa cakes	0.1	5	=B7*C7
8	doughnut	0.16	20	=B8*C8
9	packet crisps	0.46	10	=B9*C9
10	Kitkat (large pack)	2.38	5	=B10*C10
11	cola	0.97	5	=B11*C11
12	lemonade	0.97	5	=B12*C12
13	packet lollipop (5)	2.13	6	=B13*C13
14	packet balloons	0.49	2	=(B14*C14)
15			Total cost:	=SUM(D2:D14)
16			Collected:	90
17			Left to spend:	=(90-D15)

Figure 6.19 Final layout for party spreadsheet

of lemonade, but would that satisfy everyone present? You can also extend the idea by adding in entertainment or cutting down the number of people attending. The challenge is to create a realistic party for the budget available.

Spreadsheets are a very powerful data-handling tool that users can get to grips with quickly, sorting information or performing calculations. When you are creating one it saves time and effort if you know how you want to use it – the questions you want answered – before you begin. That way you will know what information to collect, how to lay it out and what formulas you will need to put into it.

Children in the younger classes will use simpler databases and graphing software, such as RM Starting Graph, Information Magic or 2Simple 2Graph. They might use 2Count to make a bar chart showing their favourite fruits (see Figure 6.20).

Or they might use 2Graph to show how many of them liked which vegetables, and they can turn their bar chart into a pie chart with the click of a button (see Figures 6.21 and 6.22).

Data logging: Monitoring the world around us

A data logging system involves a logger that records data from one or more inputs (sensors) and either displays or feeds the collected data to a computer to be viewed, analysed and stored

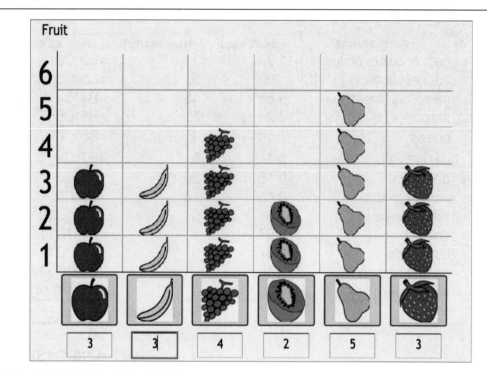

Figure 6.20 2Count showing favourite fruit

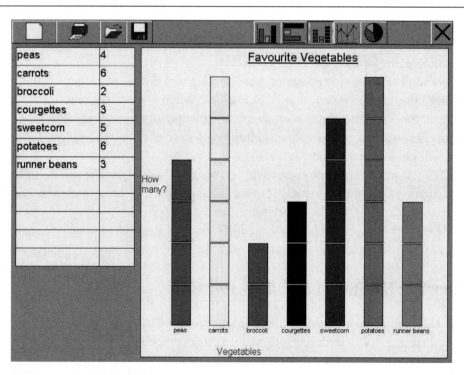

Figure 6.21 2Graph bar chart

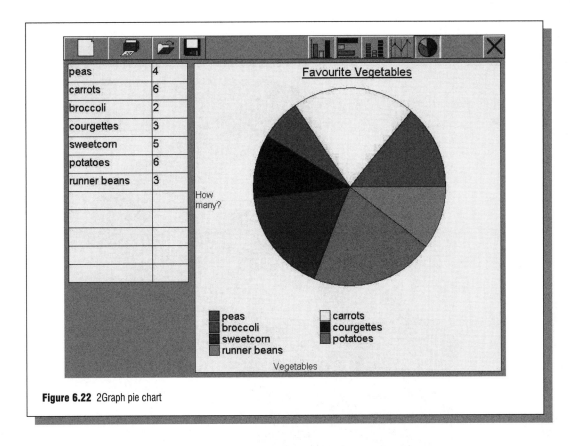

Figure 6.22 2Graph pie chart

by special software. The data can be used to produce graphs and charts. Data logging systems can capture and display data as it happens and collect data continuously or at regular intervals over long time periods (weeks, even months at a time).

Examples of data logging in the laboratory might be the measuring and recording of sound, light or temperature. Everyday use includes weather stations and traffic flow systems. Almost anything can be 'sensed' given the appropriate sensor. In school pupils will use sensors to measure light, heat, sound and temperature, but it is possible to measure all sorts of other things, such as radiation, movement and pH levels. Some data loggers would be used to control situations, by providing feedback to control systems that operate other devices– for example, a greenhouse might have a system to monitor temperature that controls the heaters or ventilation. A movement sensor can trigger an alarm.

After discussing the use of data logging in the wider world with examples of uses such as street lighting, automatic doors, seismography, measuring temperatures in museums or EEG machines to measure heart rate, a KS2 class may use data loggers as part of a science experiment to find good insulating materials. The data logger (with an attached temperature probe) can be used to record how various liquid samples cool over time, as a real-time visual display.

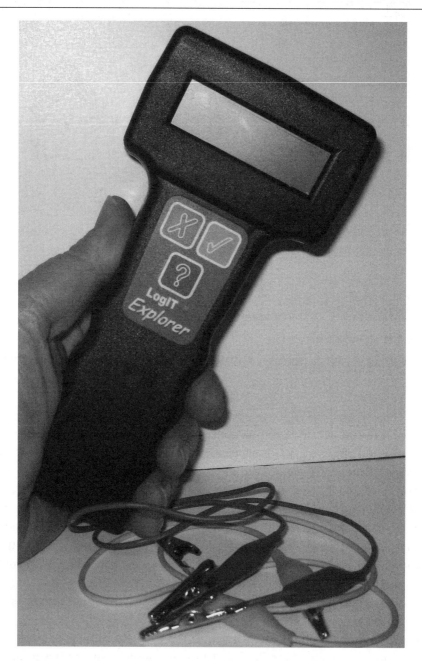

Figure 6.23 A school data logger

The class would have to learn how to attach an appropriate sensor to the data logger connected to a computer and take readings to investigate a specific question or theory. The readings would be registered on the computer and the software would compile the graphs.

The class would then use the data collected to support the science processes – hypothesising, drawing conclusions, spotting trends and patterns in results – and the children would discuss why using the data logger might be better than conventional measurements using a thermometer at timed intervals. During any activity like this the children should compare the use of ICT with other methods and decide whether ICT is always better.

Much younger children will discuss the kinds of automatic devices in everyday life that might need to sense their environment to work effectively – lift doors, street lights, automatic barriers on car parks – and categorise them (those that sense sound, those that move). They might talk about the weather, and how we measure various aspects such as temperature, rainfall, wind, cloudiness, etc. Then they might use a simple database to record weather data for several weeks and look at trends and patterns in the resulting database.

After discussing how accurate the measurements are, they could be introduced to a data logger set up to measure the environment using built in sensors (light, sound and temperature). They should compare these to human senses, and also to manual measuring equipment such as a thermometer.

With the data logger connected to the computer, the software could show who has the loudest voice or the warmest hands and see how quiet it really is when everyone is silent.

Modelling and control

Data logging and control software can be combined to develop more complex systems, both on screen and in real life. Children will learn that computer programs can be written that cause certain things to happen when certain circumstance arise and that it is possible to program a computer to control other machines and events.

Depending on the resources in schools, children might use programmable robotic or construction kits including cables and sensors for touch, light and/or sound. You might see Lego being used with a program called Robolab, and other kits might include Flowol, Junior Control Insight, CoCo and 2Control NXT. Students might design and test simple programs on screen to control a range of simple simulated control systems, such as a set of traffic lights, a lighthouse, a buggy; then they might use a control interface box with a range of inputs and outputs to allow the computer program to control a constructed 'real' version of the simulation. They will start with small sections of the system, progressing to combine them into a more complex system – such as a bumper car that they can control by programming the computer.

In the early years, children will start learning about control by using small programmable toys such as BeeBots, programmable floor robots aimed at Early Years and KS1.

When introducing floor robots or BeeBots, first of all play the 'human robot' game to remind children about instructions. Designate an adult to be the robot. Ask the children to control the robot as it moves around and goes to specific targets – 'over to the red table'. Allow children

Figure 6.24 BeeBot

to give vague/incomplete/incorrect instructions, and discuss what the robot is doing and why. Emphasise to the children the need to be clear and precise in their instructions and the sequencing of them. Work together to 'program' the robot correctly, using simple direction and distance vocabulary. Introduce the idea of giving several instructions that are 'stored' in the robot 'memory' and then all done at once when you say 'GO'.

As well as actually playing with and learning about the floor robot or BeeBot, the children can try programming an onscreen turtle. Using the programme on the school network (perhaps Softease Turtle, Logo or 2Go), the onscreen turtle can be programmed to go for a walk.

This screenshot from 2Go from 2Simple Software shows arrows for forward and backward, turn left and turn right. As with similar programs, it can be easily altered to give arrows for diagonals, to remove the need for distance, or to follow a flow diagram (the 'teacher's option' **Ctrl + Shift + O** gives you the other options). Different backgrounds can also be used to provide different challenges.

Here the car has been programmed to travel from the pink house to the red one. The steps can be watched as the program runs and then quickly edited.

These programs lend themselves to setting different challenges for pupils of different abilities. While you might ask one child to draw a square, you might ask another to draw a series of

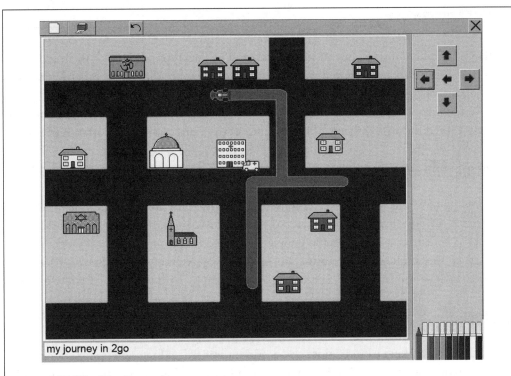

Figure 6.25 Using 2Go with arrow keys

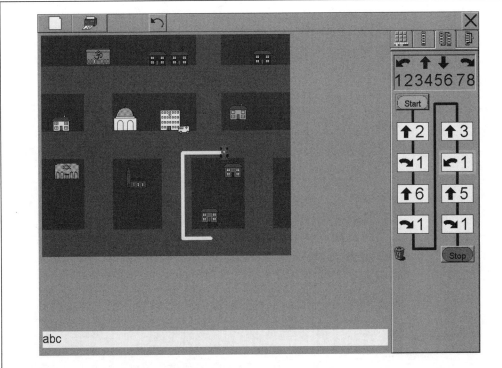

Figure 6.26 Using 2Go with programming flowchart

squares of different sizes, one inside the other. The backgrounds will let them guide the turtle from one place to another, and they can move on to more difficult geometric shapes, such as hexagons, or to teach the computer to write their initials.

While this is still a long way from learning the code to create their own games, they will have learned the basic process of sequencing instructions and the importance of precision.

Gathering and working with data online

Knowing how and where to search online is important for anyone using the internet for their research. Choose the right database and then learn what search terms work best. If we want specific information from specific people – say feedback from a trip or a workshop – we can create our own questionnaire using an online survey website such as Survey Monkey, which lets us analyse the answers and create charts and graphs with the click of a few buttons.

Conclusion

Computers can help us to explore the world by using data logging equipment and to control it through programming. Models or simulations help us find things out and solve problems in a wide range of real and imaginary situations, so children can explore options, make choices and test predictions. Pupils will apply what they have learned throughout their work.

7

Presenting ideas

Computers make it possible quickly and easily to put together presentations that combine images, text, sound and video – what we know as multimedia authoring. You will have seen PowerPoint presentations, where text flies in from all angles accompanied by sound effects, and lists of bullet points will drop into place to emphasise a point the speaker is making. Such programs can be used to create other sorts of resources quickly and easily, such as books and websites.

Where once they just did writing, now pupils, even in KS1, also create presentations as a means of expressing themselves. Pupils can find this liberating as they can use other media, such as sound, video and images, to get their message across.

Teaching assistants may find that one of the ways they will be supporting classes is by creating resources to use on the interactive whiteboard (IWB). It is well worth getting to know Microsoft PowerPoint, one of the quickest and easiest ways to make interactive resources, but which can also be used to make books and leaflets. The chart facility will instantly create a graph more simply than Excel.

Creating presentations with PowerPoint

You may find that you are creating presentations as part of a curriculum project, as a tool for teaching or to inform people (such as at a parents' evening) about a proposed school journey. Whichever, the process is the same.

The activity described below applies ICT skills to a science project on 'Space'. In a class activity, different pupils or groups of pupils could be allocated specific topics such as 'The Planets' or 'Living in Space' – these can later be linked together using 'hyperlinks'.

When you first open PowerPoint it will probably start directly with a new presentation. (If you have an older version of the program it may ask if you want to start a new presentation or open an existing one, in which case you will need to choose the former to get a first slide on screen.) Whenever you start a new presentation it will offer you a title slide, as shown in Figure 7.1.

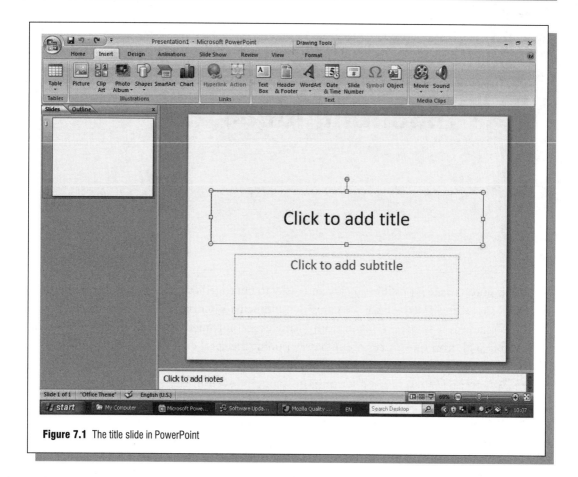

Figure 7.1 The title slide in PowerPoint

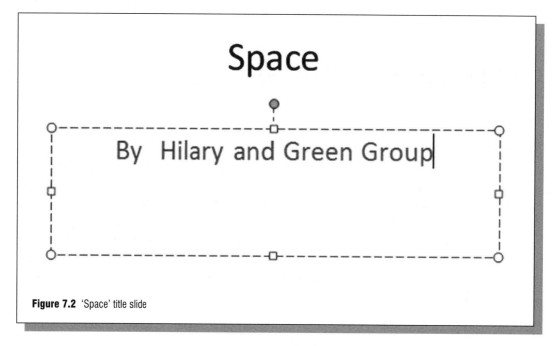

Figure 7.2 'Space' title slide

This page is a 'Template'. PowerPoint has many of these to help you. On the left you can choose to see thumbnails of your slides, or an outline of the points added so far. As you can see, you can simply click on a box and type to begin. Here we can type 'Space' and 'by Hilary and Green Group' (see Figure 7.2).

We can also add colour and animations. These can be on individual objects, the graphics and text boxes you create, or for the whole slide.

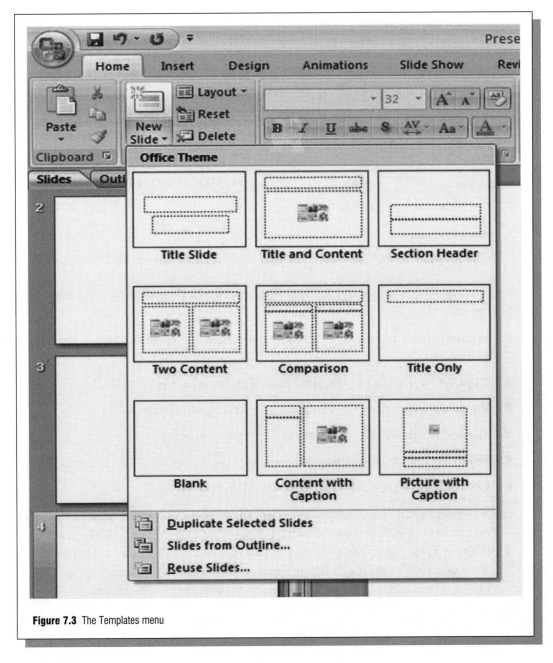

Figure 7.3 The Templates menu

To add a second slide follow **Home > New Slide**. Click on the tiny arrow next to the words **New Slide** and the available templates will appear, either as a new dialog box on screen or as a sidebar (depending on which version of PowerPoint you are using). These have predetermined spaces for bullet points, graphics, graphs and even sound and video clips. Figure 7.3 is a selection of those available in PowerPoint 2007.

If you choose the blank slide you can add whatever you want. As with all programs, there are a number of ways of performing the same task and you will learn the ones that suit you best; however, as you will see, with PowerPoint most of what you will want to do can be found under the Insert menu.

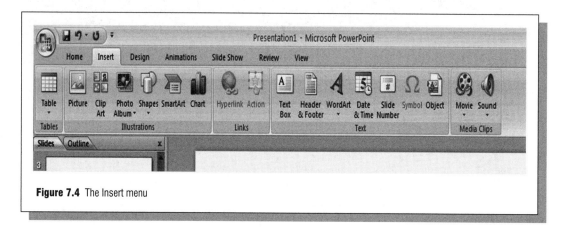

Figure 7.4 The Insert menu

From this illustration you can see that when you choose the **Insert** tab you have the options to choose:

- **Picture**, which are graphics that you have created and saved somewhere, such as photos or drawings

- **Clip Art**, which are graphics that come with the program

- **Photo Album**, which lets you quickly make an onscreen album

- **Shapes**, which are such things as stars and speech bubbles

- **SmartArt**, which are graphics that let you create a diagram of several levels

- **Chart**, which creates charts to illustrate and compare data.

Other items you can insert include WordArt, which is decorative text in your document.

The first slide of my presentation will be about 'The Planets' and to add impact it will use WordArt for a title. Choosing this from the **Insert** menu brings up this dialog box. (Note that WordArt may vary according to the program and version you are using.)

You select the style of title, and then enter your caption into the box on the slide (see Figure 7.6).

From the toolbar above you can re-format the title, changing font style and colour, or adding a 3D effect, such as a shadow and so on.

To add an image to illustrate the subject open the **Insert** tab and choose the source, in this case **Clip Art**. What appears will again depend on your version of PowerPoint. In the 2007 sidebar you will type a search term into the 'Search text' box (see Figure 7.7).

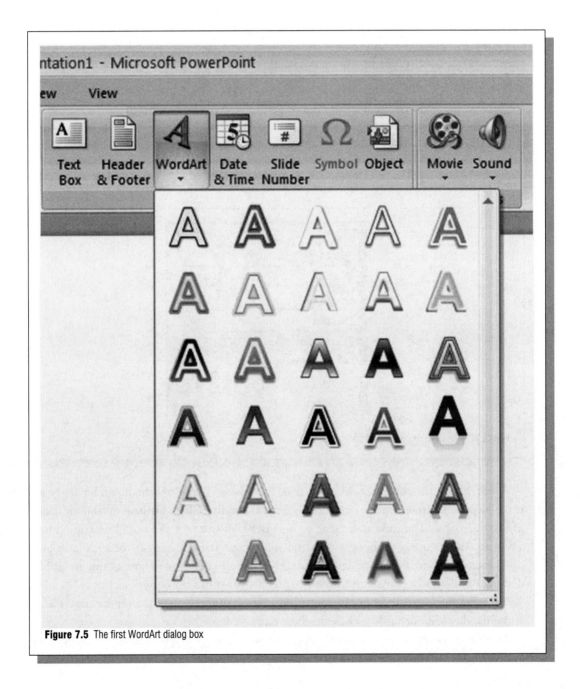

Figure 7.5 The first WordArt dialog box

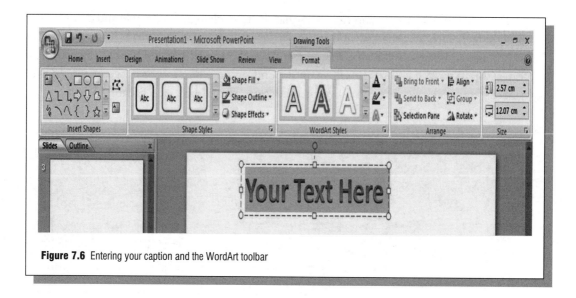

Figure 7.6 Entering your caption and the WordArt toolbar

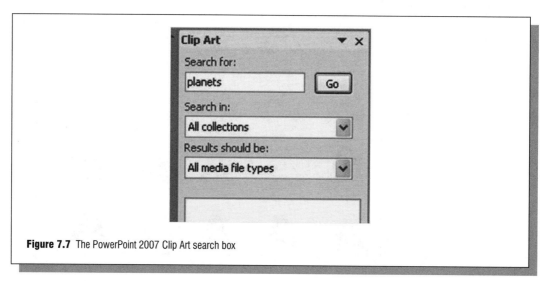

Figure 7.7 The PowerPoint 2007 Clip Art search box

A search for 'planets' may find more than forty images, any of which can be easily inserted. It is also possible to use images from the internet, and the **Clips Online** option (at the bottom of the sidebar) will automatically search the Microsoft site or a clip could be copied following a search. When using an image from the internet it is important to observe any copyright restrictions, and to acknowledge the source, particularly if you are going to publish the document as a book or website. (See Chapter 14 for more on copyright.)

Once inserted, the object can be moved, or resized using the handles on the edges, or rotated. If the handles are not visible, click on the object once.

As you move the cursor over the object it will change shape as different options become available.

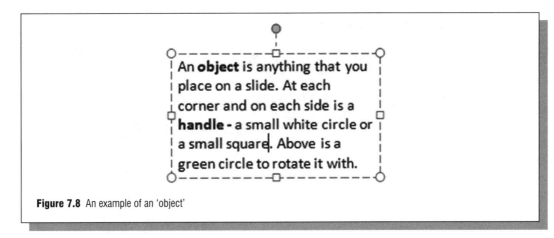

Figure 7.8 An example of an 'object'

- The normal cursor will change to

- the **move** cursor, which looks like this

- or the **re-size** cursor, available when over a **handle**, like this

- and the **rotate** cursor, which looks like this

To add writing a **Text Box** can be added, again from the **Insert** tab. The text can be formatted just as in a word processor.

You can also change the colour scheme of the slide from the **Design** tab, either using a **Theme**, which offers lots of different professional-looking layouts, or by using **Background Style > Format Background**, which changes the colour of either one slide or all of them and allows you to put a picture as your background. This can transform the presentation instantly into something more interesting (see Figures 7.9, 7.10 and 7.11).

When all the slides have been completed, the presentation can be viewed through three routes: by following **Slide Show > From Beginning**; by pressing **F5** on the keyboard; or by clicking on the **Slide Show** button at the bottom left of the screen (see Figure 7.12).

The other views available include 'Normal', which shows the layout of the slide and the contents in sidebar to the left (as in Figure 7.12), and 'Slide Sorter', which shows them as a storyboard so that you can move them around to change the order.

When viewing a show, slides are advanced by clicking the mouse button, the space bar, the enter key or by using the navigation arrows on the keyboard. This is akin to turning the pages of a book. However, another way of moving between slides, in a non-linear manner, is to use hyperlinks. These work like links on the internet, where you click on a word, sentence or object and jump to another place. In the 'Space' presentation it could be a jump:

- to a list of the planets
- from the name of a planet to a slide with particular information about it
- to a website.

Figure 7.9 This slide has an unformatted background

Figure 7.10 This slide has a gradient fill effect applied

Figure 7.11 A slide with a design applied

Figure 7.12 The presentation view options

Hyperlinks can again be accessed through the **Insert** tab options, by clicking on **Hyperlink**. First of all, the object or text to be linked needs to be highlighted. With text, this is done in the usual way by holding down the left mouse button and running the cursor over the text. With an object, this is done by clicking to make it active – that is, with its 'handles' showing. The Insert Hyperlink dialog box is shown in Figure 7.13.

There are a number of options for links. One is to link to any document on the computer, another is to link to a website by entering an internet address. You can also create links between slides. To link the word 'planets' from the second slide to a list of them would require clicking on the **Place in this document** option (see Figure 7.14).

A preview is shown of the available slides. The hyperlink is created by simply selecting the slide to link to and clicking **OK**.

When using hyperlinks it may be necessary to switch off the automatic page turning, this can be done by following **Animations > Advance Slide > On Mouse Click**, and making sure the box is unchecked. Now slides are not automatically opened at the click of a mouse

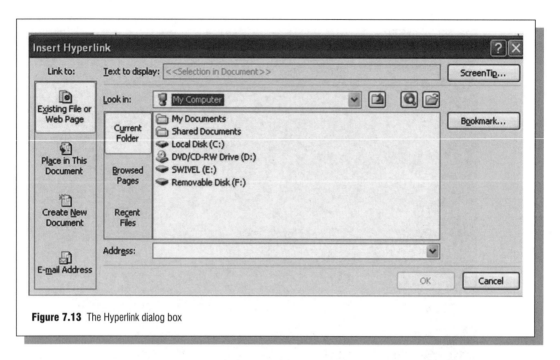

Figure 7.13 The Hyperlink dialog box

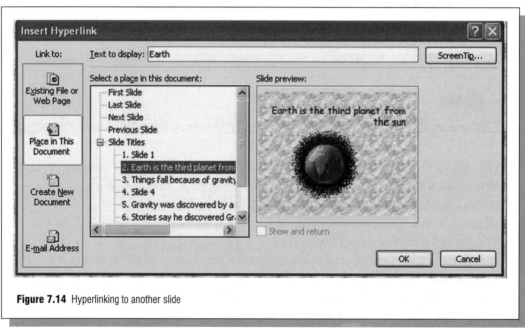

Figure 7.14 Hyperlinking to another slide

or key but only when linked to. When a hyperlink is present on a slide the cursor will change to the 'browser finger' when it passes over it: . Any text links will be underlined and, as on a webpage, may change colour once they have been followed.

This interactivity means that PowerPoint can be used to create websites. Simply follow **Office Button > Save as type > Web Page**, and it will automatically format the pages and their content for use on a website. This will also allow the presentation to be viewed in web-browsing software such as Internet Explorer. Apart from posting on the internet, this option can also allow pupils to take copies home to view when they do not have PowerPoint on their own machines. However, another option is to use **Package for CD**, in the **Office Button > Publish** menu, as this adds a 'viewer' to the presentation so it can be used on any machine.

Presentations can also be printed out and used as books. By selecting **View > Handouts** the number of slides per page can be set at anything from one to nine. Choosing two slides to a page makes an A5 booklet, using four or more can give a comic strip effect. This could be used with clipart or photos and speech bubbles to create books such as stories or collections of jokes.

To add speech bubbles to a slide follow **Insert > Shapes** and then choose the speech bubbles from the **Callouts**. These can be altered as with any object. Text is inserted by simply typing when the object is active, and the background colour can be changed by using the fill bucket on the **Format** tab (as discussed in Chapter 5). This becomes visible when you double click the shape.

It is also quite straightforward to add sounds. These can be from the available library or easily recorded. To do this follow **Insert > Movies** or **> Sounds**, then choose one of the

Figure 7.15 Using graphics and speech bubbles

options. If you choose **Record Sound** you can record your voice and make a talking book. The text could be read as you open the page, or by clicking on the speaker icon that appears.

You can even attach the sound to an object so that it is activated by clicking on it. This is one of the **Custom Animations** to be found in the **Animation** tab menu. Here you may also click on **Slide Transition**, which allows you to decide how one slide changes to the next.

There are other options, such as **Slide Show > Rehearse Timings**, which automatically moves the presentation on after a given time. This is useful if you are going to have it running for people to view, perhaps playing a looping introduction to the school in the reception area.

With a few relatively simple techniques you can create quite sophisticated resources, combining text, images and even sounds to good effect. Hyperlinks will let you create tools such as quizzes to use in class, or adventure stories where the reader chooses which path to follow. The use of speech bubbles and pupils' own voices can create books where they literally read to themselves, and the printing options mean your creations can be appreciated away from the computer as well as on it.

Creating presentations with younger children using 2Create a Story

2Simple's 2Create a Story is popular in many primary schools as it has an easy-to-use interface, not too much text and children in Foundation Stage and KS1 can make talking stories in minutes and publish them almost anywhere. They can combine words, pictures, sounds and animation in a storybook format to publish literacy, science, history, RE and other work. This program allows them to animate their drawings, include pre-recorded, or their own, noises and save their work as a flash file that can then be shown on the internet or any other computer or as a file that can be printed out as a fold up storybook.

To open the software click on **2Create a Story** and you will find a window divided in two with colourful felt-tip pen tools down the side (see Figure 7.16).

Children can select a thin or a fat felt tip pen and draw their picture. In the box below they can write their text. Using the buttons at the top of the screen they can alter the size of the font, animate their picture, add a sound effect or record their own sounds. To animate their picture they should click on the **red fish** and from the dropdown menu select the animation. Remember the whole picture will be animated; you cannot animate just selected parts of the picture. See Figure 7.17.

From the dropdown menu on the grey speaker button they can select a special effect, select a sound file from the computer or record their own voice or effect. The keyboard button gives a piano/organ/keyboard upon which they can compose and record their own background sound (see Figure 7.18).

It is important to remember the teacher's options, which are found by clicking **Ctrl + Shift + O** at the same time. Here you can change the tools, fonts, folder and printer options. You can choose whether to show the animation button and the undo button. The print button prints four pages on each piece of paper. These can be folded up to make a little book.

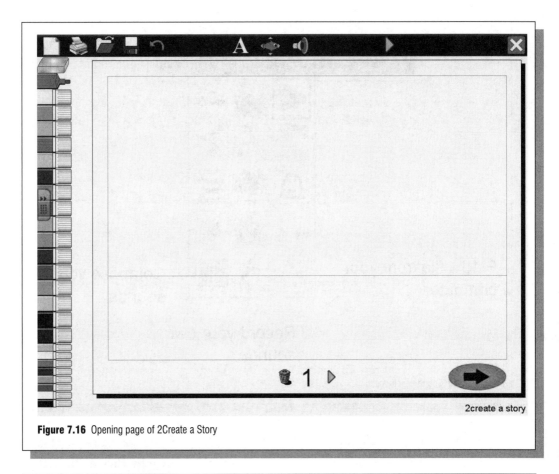

Figure 7.16 Opening page of 2Create a Story

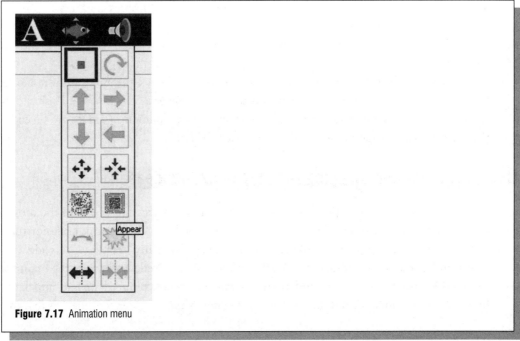

Figure 7.17 Animation menu

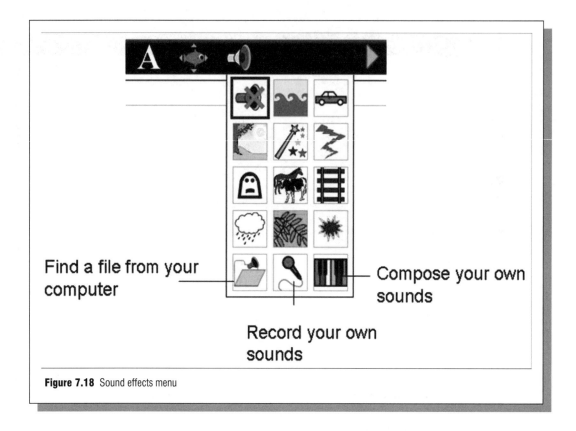

Figure 7.18 Sound effects menu

If you have chosen the more sophisticated set of tools (called 'Tools' as opposed to 'Classic Tools') then you have an option to import pictures of your own by clicking the right mouse button on the painting section to bring up a copy, paste and import menu.

Use **Copy** and **Paste** to copy pictures from one page to another and import pictures, photographs or even your own animated GIF files from 2Animate using the **Import** option.

Either save and print out your story as a little book or click the **Save** button and tick the **SWF** box at the bottom of the screen; this saves your file as a Shock Wave Flash file that can then be viewed in an internet browser or emailed as an attachment. (Videos are provided with the software to provide demonstrations of how to use it.)

Using concept/mind-mapping software to gather ideas

The technique of mind mapping® was created by Tony Buzan and is one of the most widely used thinking tools around the world. It has been called the 'Swiss army knife for the brain', because it is a multi-purpose thinking tool and is used by many people worldwide.

A mind map or concept map is a visual thinking tool that reflects the way the brain naturally thinks. On mind maps, ideas and thoughts are shown as coloured images and key words branching out from a central theme. One of the key benefits of concept maps is that they help

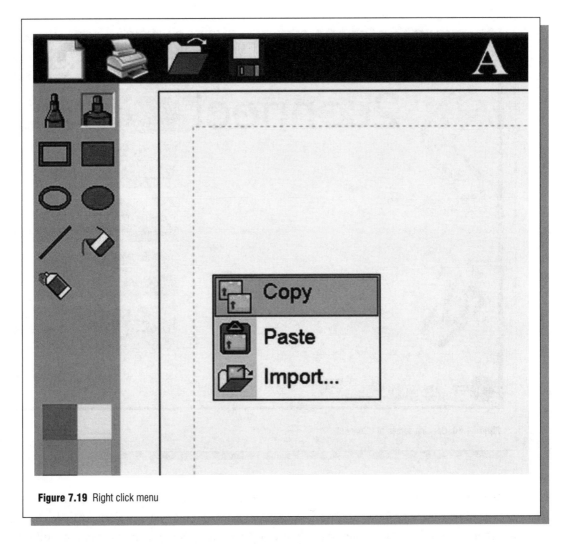

Figure 7.19 Right click menu

you see how ideas link to each other as well as how they relate to the central theme. Research shows that visual learning is one of the best methods for teaching thinking skills. Visual learning techniques – graphical ways of working with ideas and planning and presenting information – teach students to clarify their thinking and to process, organise and prioritise new information.

Frequently used concept-mapping software in schools includes Inspiration, Kidspiration and 2Simple's 2Connect.

You could, for example, work on a 'Healthy Eating' topic using 2Connect. The options on the opening page are shown in Figure 7.20.

Start a new file and begin to gather suggestions of food from the children. If you are using this on the interactive whiteboard the children can come and write ideas themselves on the board. (Remember that **Ctrl + Shift + O** gives you the teacher's options, where there is a whiteboard 'string' that can be added to the screen and used to pull the 2Connect screen down for shorter pupils.)

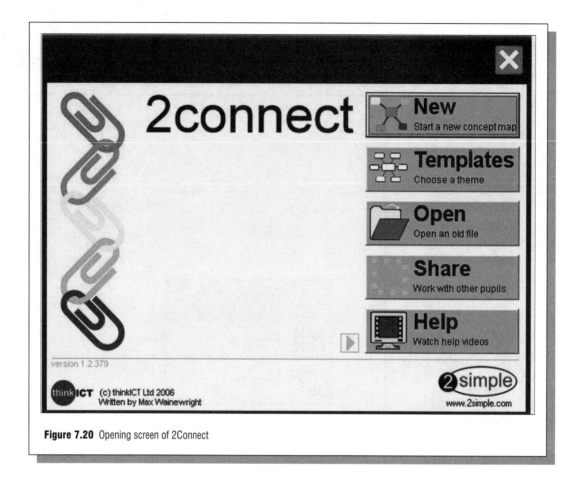

Figure 7.20 Opening screen of 2Connect

When a word is typed, suggested clipart will appear. Click on the image you want to use, and it will be inserted into the idea box. To link idea boxes, you can drag one idea box over another and a link will form between them, or place the cursor at edge of idea box and a pencil icon will appear. Drag the pencil over to the box to which you wish to link.

To delete any linking line, select it and press **Delete** on the keyboard. To re-link one end of a line to a different idea box, click on the line to select it, then click on the square at the end of the line and drag it to the box to which you wish to link it. Right-click on a line to change its colour, the direction of the arrowhead or to remove the arrowhead.

To edit an ideas box, click on the button at the top of the screen, which opens a dropdown menu. Click on a button to choose the colour of the selected idea box or click on the bottom button for more advanced options. (You can also edit any idea box by right clicking on it.)

In the edit box you can paint a picture, choose a picture from clipart or import a picture from elsewhere on your computer. This (copyright free) picture was searched for with Google image search, saved to **My Computer** and then inserted.

The middle tab at the bottom of the edit screen allows you to change the font and the colours of the idea box. The third tab allows you to write notes for an idea box that will appear when

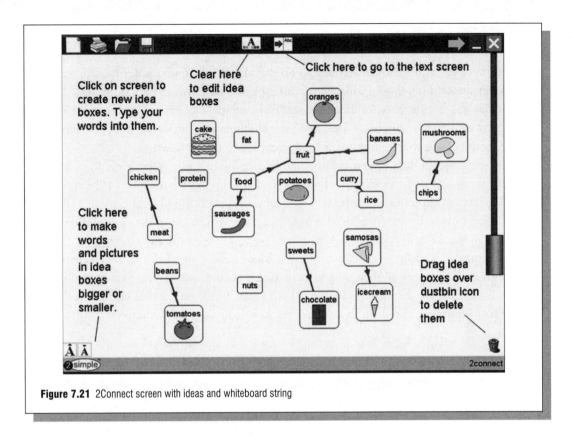

Figure 7.21 2Connect screen with ideas and whiteboard string

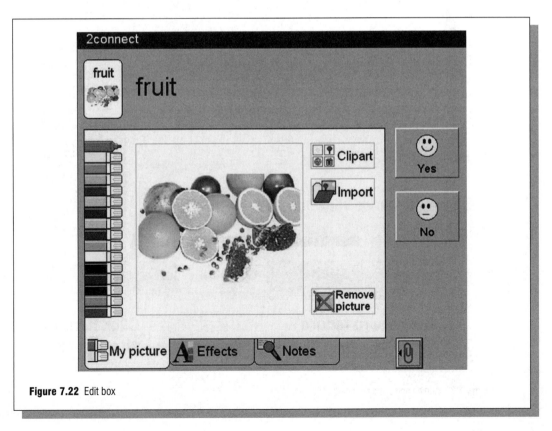

Figure 7.22 Edit box

you hover your cursor over that box. You can also record audio notes to help to remind you of your ideas (though you will need a microphone attached to the computer). On this page you can attach a file to your idea box, such as a recipe for samosas, as here (see Figure 7.23).

After gathering examples of food from the children you can decide together what categories the foods belong to from the main food groups (see Figure 7.24).

By clicking the text screen button (see Figure 7.21) you can click on the idea boxes and your words and pictures will appear in the box on the right-hand side of the screen.

The class or group may use the map as a support for writing or now present their ideas using the concept map by selecting an idea box that they wish to use as the central theme or starting point (in this case 'Food') by clicking on it. Next, click on the **green arrow** at the top right of the main screen to access the dropdown menu, and then click on the **Present my ideas** option at the bottom to open up a presentation screen. Click on the plus symbols to open the links, and click on the minuses to close them again. Click on the **red square** at the top of the screen to return to the main 2Connect screen to edit your presentation.

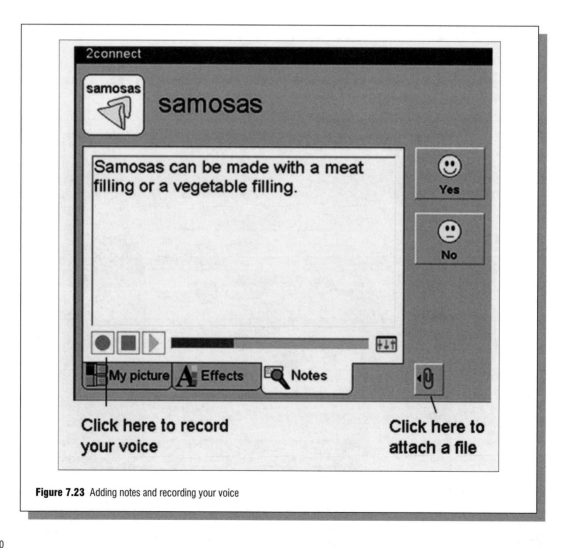

Figure 7.23 Adding notes and recording your voice

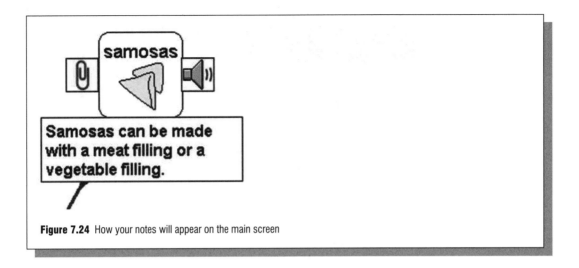

Figure 7.24 How your notes will appear on the main screen

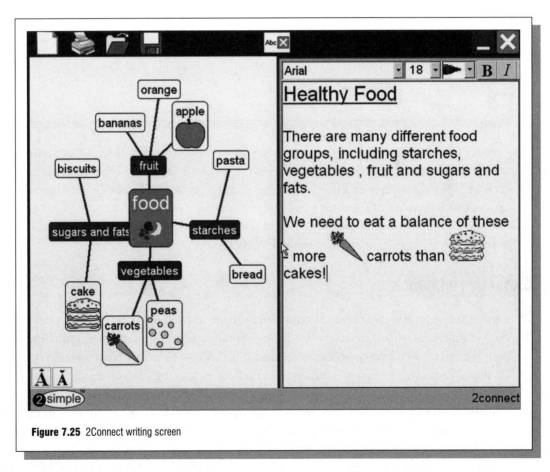

Figure 7.25 2Connect writing screen

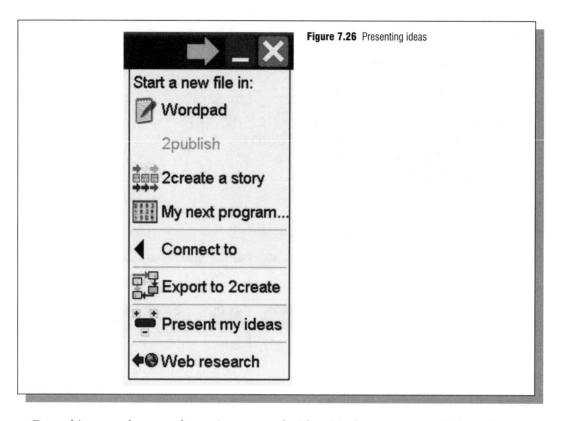

Figure 7.26 Presenting ideas

From this menu there are also options to use the ideas in other programs. Click on the **green arrow** to get the menu. You can embed your words and images in other 2Simple programs such as 2Create a Story (see above). You can connect to Word, Publisher or Paint and open up your web browser to continue your research.

Other concept-mapping software, such as Kidspiration, might be used in school. Here is an example of the same kind of work done in Kidspiration (see Figure 7.27).

Interactive whiteboards

Opportunities for presentation and communication are opened up by an IWB, allowing whole-class engagement with interactive teaching programs, websites, video clips and the use of peripherals such as microscopes and webcams. It is also easy to demonstrate specific skills, such as editing a scanned-in draft of a student's work. This is done by controlling the software using a pointer/pen (or finger) on the whiteboard screen and annotating the text.

Good use of the interactive whiteboard incorporates a variety of teaching techniques that support a range of preferred learning styles, including visual, auditory and kinaesthetic learning, and many classrooms have them (see Chapter 1).

Obviously the whiteboard can be used as a large computer display to demonstrate to a class something that is on the computer to which it is connected, but there are other uses for interactive whiteboards:

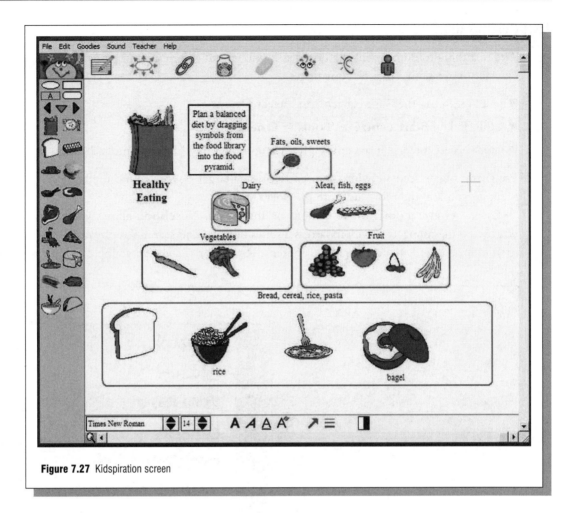

Figure 7.27 Kidspiration screen

- the use of in-built software to capture notes written on it
- translating cursive writing to text (not all whiteboards can do this)
- The interactive whiteboard may be provided with an integrated audience response system (ARS) so presenters can carry out polls and quizzes and capture the feedback on the whiteboard software.

Popular whiteboards in schools include Promethean and SMART boards. We will look here at some of the things you can do with a SMART board, but other whiteboard software will have similar applications.

Basic troubleshooting

If you can see the image on the laptop/desktop computer, but not the projector, make sure it is turned on and then press **Fn** and **F5** (or sometimes **F8**, depending on the computer) at the same time. You might need to press it more than once to show the image on both screens.

Orientating the board

The first thing to do is orient the board as it will go out of orientation periodically, making it difficult to use with a pen or your finger.

- EITHER use the Task bar icon and select **Orient**
- OR follow **Start centre > Tools > Orient**
- OR access the orient screen by pressing both pen tray buttons simultaneously.

Press your finger accurately into the centre of each target – work round the board. The more accurate you are, the more accurate the board will be.

There are several other useful buttons on this menu. **Notebook** allows you to save notes written on the interactive whiteboard as a series of pages and search for objects in the Gallery, such as images, video and interactive content. **Recorder** records all action that take place on

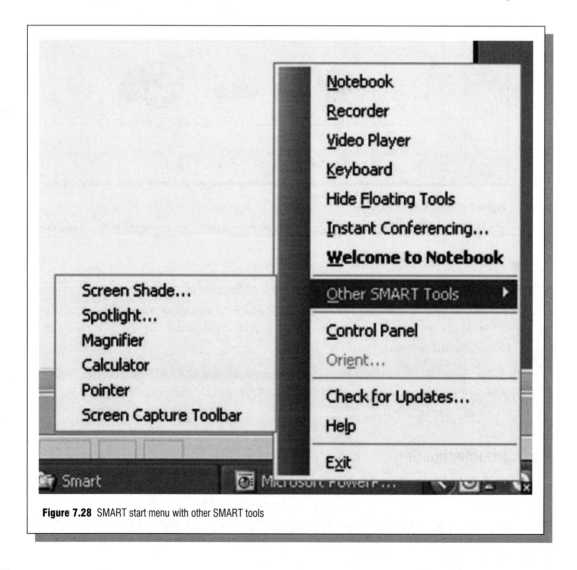

Figure 7.28 SMART start menu with other SMART tools

your interactive whiteboard, such as training processes, and allows you to add audio with a microphone, control quality and video format and share your recording with colleagues. **Video Player** allows you to write or draw over video during a presentation. Use the SMART video player to play files located on your computer or view content from a camera, VCR, CD-ROM or DVD. **Keyboard** allows you to type or edit any text in any application without leaving the interactive whiteboard.

Floating Tools give you a toolbar from which you can quickly access pens, highlighters and other frequently used tools, take screen captures, undo or redo an action on your interactive whiteboard and customise the Floating Tools toolbar. As you hover over the buttons on the floating toolbar a small label tells you what each button is.

Other SMART tools

From the menu on the task bar you can access other SMART tools. Very useful with younger children is the **Spotlight** tool. This can be used to focus on one particular area of the screen – for example, you could spotlight just one part of a picture of an animal and the children can try and guess what the creature is behind when you are revealing only that one small area.

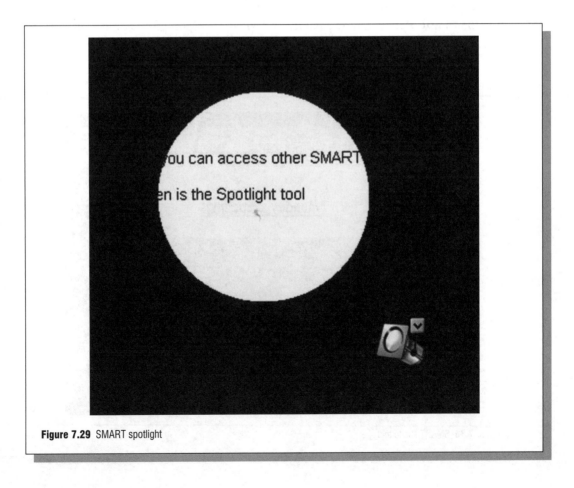

Figure 7.29 SMART spotlight

The **Screen Shade** tool could also be useful when checking answers to a quiz, a test or yesterday's spellings (see Figure 7.30).

The magnifier can be useful for enlarging small text or images to make them easier to see. (Two windows appear; the smaller one is used to select the area you would like to magnify and the larger one displays the magnified view. See Figure 7.31.)

The **Screen Capture Toolbar** allows you to capture a selected area, window or a full screengrab from your desktop. The captured image will automatically appear as a page in your Notebook file.

Using the SMART notebook software

Start by loading the Smart Notebook (**Start > All Programs > SMART Notebook software**).

Play around to get used to what the board and the software do. Use the pens (or take a pen out and use a finger/paintbrush). Try moving/resizing/rotating objects (tap on them, drag them around – the white circle resizes and the green circle rotates). Use the rubber (rub out normally, or draw a circle and tap in the middle to make things vanish).

The toolbars are shown in Figures 7.32 and 7.33.

Try the **Magic Pen** and draw a circle/oval to create a spotlight that hides other parts of the screen; draw a square/rectangle to create a magnifying tool to enlarge areas or write/draw other shapes to annotate – your annotations will fade away after a few seconds.

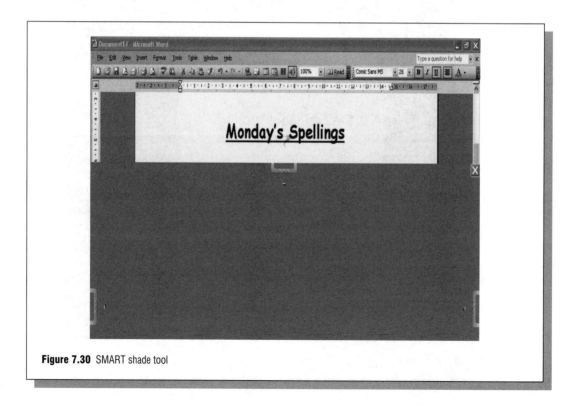

Figure 7.30 SMART shade tool

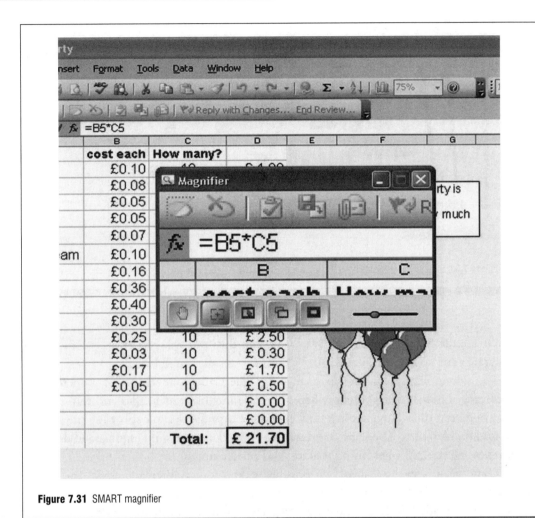

Figure 7.31 SMART magnifier

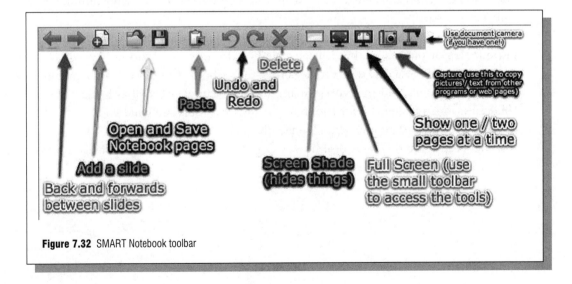

Figure 7.32 SMART Notebook toolbar

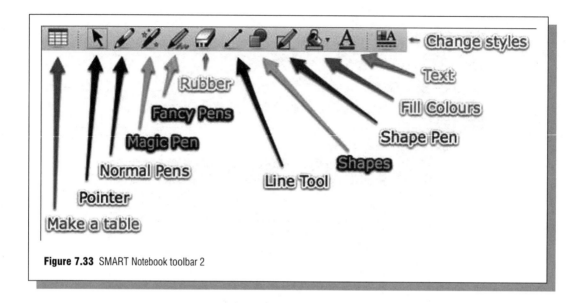

Figure 7.33 SMART Notebook toolbar 2

Or use the **Shape Pen** to draw a shape, and this tool will recognise it and draw it more accurately for you (see Figure 7.34).

The side toolbar gives you the page sorter, the Gallery, attachments, properties and page recording. Look in the **Gallery** where there are lots of great images and tools that you can drag and drop onto the notebook. Either browse through the folders or use the search facility to find backgrounds. There are interactive tools such as timers, maps, drag and drop activities, puzzles and so on for lessons right across the curriculum.

Using what is in the Gallery it is possible to find tools and create lessons and activities for many subjects. But there are also many interactive whiteboard lessons on the internet, ready to be downloaded. SMART board lessons can be found on http://exchange.smarttech.com/ but lesson activities can also be found for Promethean boards at www.prometheanplanet.com/en/.

Ideas can be presented in a variety of ways using multimedia tools. The audience might be just our class or our school, but it is possible now to show our work to the whole world by publishing online – and it is so simple to do. Our school websites can be showcases for the ideas we are having and the work we are doing in school. As well as being a showcase for children's work and giving information to parents, governors and children, they can have links to our school radio station or school video channel.

Other chapters in this book deal how we can learn to use these multimedia tools and what is available online to support our learning.

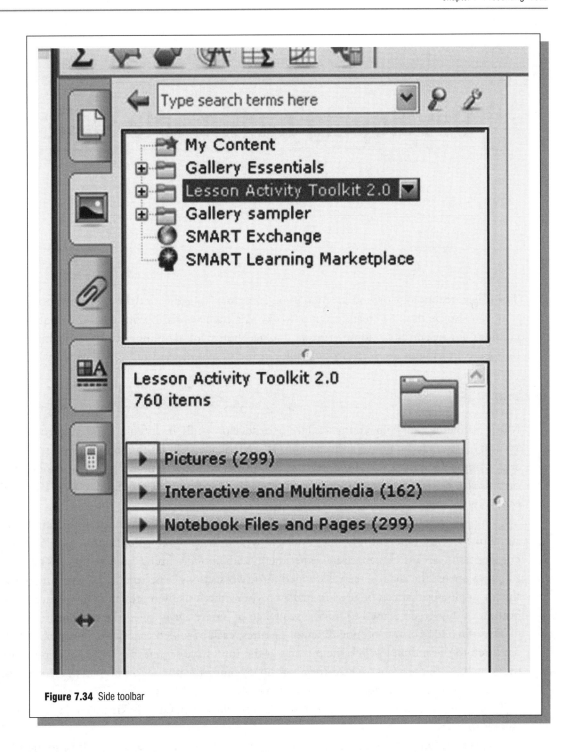

Figure 7.34 Side toolbar

8

Developing multimedia skills

The role of technology extends beyond using computers to gather and disseminate information; they can also be used to create original works to a high standard, with even the youngest of children, for instance, composing music, taking photos and designing radio programmes and film animations with the software available for use in school.

Making music

Music activities can help young children to develop skills in listening and concentration, communication and physical coordination, as well as laying down the foundation for reading and writing. In school, children will use computers to create musical patterns, choose and organise sounds and develop musical ideas. They should also be able to listen to their own and others' work and suggest improvements.

Compose World Play is a program for creating compositions from musical phrases. There are about seventy different tune files available within the program. Pupils can create and edit compositions, and they can easily experiment with mood, timings and tempo. When the program opens, the main screen is divided into two sections. The top of the screen contains the list of phrases that can be used to make up your tune, usually represented by pictures. The bottom of the screen is used to build a sequence of phrases. It is called the sequencer.

The initial file consists of nine different pictures, each of which represents a musical phrase. To listen to them double-click the pictures at the top of the screen. To make a composition, move a phrase to the sequencer by dragging and dropping the phrase to a box on the sequencer, repeating to construct a sequence of musical phrases.

To play the sequence, click the **green arrow** and adjust tempo by clicking the tempo buttons (**black arrows**) up or down.

An exercise linked to literacy, RE or history might be to compose a portrait in sound of a character for a story or a situation and give the children three or four boxes (**View > Sequence > Options** and change the grid to one row of three or four). Ask them to choose sounds similar or related to their subject. Children might make jingles – for a presentation or to use in their podcasts between news items. (You will need to choose **Make a midi file** in the **File** menu for this, otherwise you will not be able to embed the jingle in PowerPoint, Publisher or a web page, or import it into Audacity.)

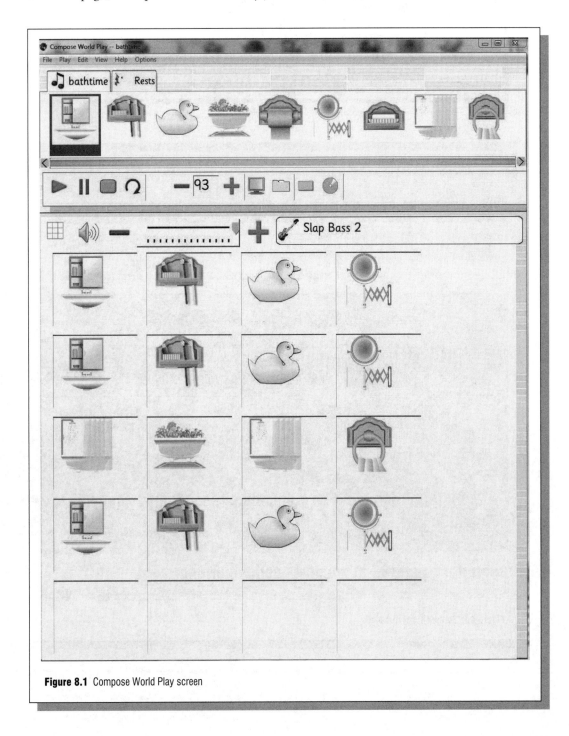

Figure 8.1 Compose World Play screen

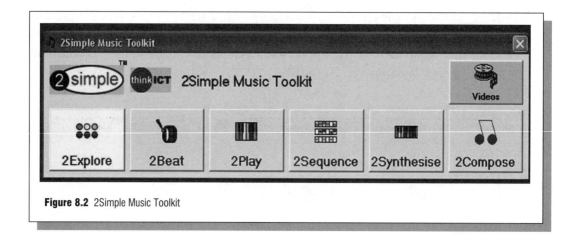

Figure 8.2 2Simple Music Toolkit

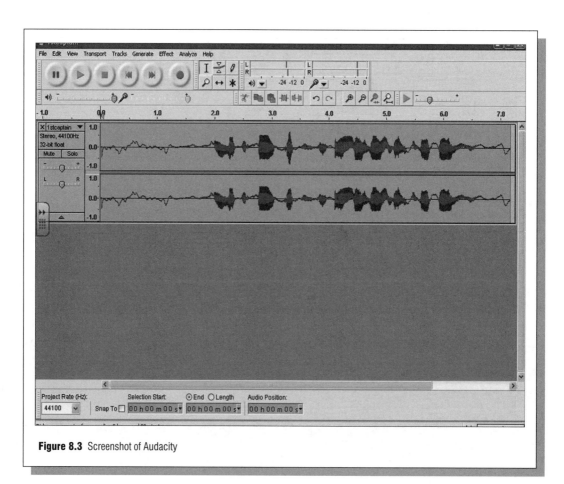

Figure 8.3 Screenshot of Audacity

Another popular piece of music-making software is 2Simple's Music Toolkit, which is a suite of six music programs that can be used to develop music capability across Foundation Stage, KS1 and KS2. It allows children to investigate a range of musical concepts, from creating simple sequences of sounds and investigating rhythms to composing short pieces of music to add to web pages or presentations. When you click on the **Music Toolkit** icon, a suite of programs opens: 2Explore, 2Beat, 2Play, 2Sequence, 2Synthesise and 2Compose.

Make use of the excellent **Videos** (the link on the top right-hand side of the menu), which teach the viewer how to use each of the programs and gives ideas for curricular use.

Many schools have Audacity, a multi-track editing tool that is great for those starting out with digital audio, podcasting, or learning about audio recording. It is possible to use it on stand alone computers and on networks.

With any musical activities carried out, the issue of noise distracting neighbouring groups needs to be considered. If headphones are available, they can help in both the classroom and computer room, but for group activities multiple headphones would need to be connected to the same computer. If you have multimedia speakers on the computer, make sure they are pointing away from other groups.

Note that at KS3 and above, ICT is embedded in the music curriculum and not taught as a separate ICT unit.

Digital photography

The opportunity to take, use, develop and share photos is now commonplace in most pupils' lives, with the coming of low-cost digital cameras and the inclusion of a camera on most mobile phones. Photography can be used across the curriculum in easy and creative ways. Photos can extend the life of children's Lego models beyond the period of the lesson in which they were constructed, and then they can be provided as evidence of progress for teachers and proud parents.

Photos can be used to aid documentation of experiments in science, to support storytelling or in the teaching of modern foreign languages. They can also be used in lessons for activities such as sequencing. Even long-term projects such as growing beans or watching tadpoles become frogs can be recorded step by step.

Cameras taken on field trips and outings can take photos for the school website, wall displays, presentations to assemblies and plenary sessions. They can be used by teaching assistants to record a child's small steps in achievement through P level targets, which might otherwise be difficult to describe.

Using digital cameras

There are a very wide range of cameras on the market, ranging in price and quality, and it is possible to buy cameras specifically built for children, made of tough plastic with big buttons

– but careful thought needs to be given to how simple or otherwise a camera is to use. Getting the photos off the camera needs to be straightforward. Most cameras connect directly to the computer via a special lead, and the camera will appear as a separate drive in the 'My Computer' folder on the desktop. The pictures can be simply dragged and dropped into another folder on the computer.

Still images

There are a number of things the pupils can do with their photos. One is to edit and enhance them. For this, specialist software such as Adobe Photoshop is useful, although most painting programs will open these images, so MS Paint and RM Colour Magic will let pupils change the look of their photos. The example below is from photo editing software called Photo Simple, which enables photo editing and enhancement with a very easy-to-use interface for even the youngest children. The children can apply special effects and print out their pictures.

Figure 8.4 The same photo modified in different ways

Photo albums

PowerPoint helps you make an album easily, with added captions, speech bubbles and backgrounds, which can be a simple way to create a storybook. 2Create a Story can be similarly used make books, either printed out on paper or saved and viewed on a computer.

Still images can be used alone, embedded in documents or presentations, made into collages (look at the Picnik website) and panoramas (look at the Clevr website); or they can very effectively be brought to life by importing them into movie-making software such as Movie Maker, Animoto and Photo Story 3.

Photo stories

Photo Story 3 has easy-to-follow prompts to help you upload your images, edit them and add subtitles, effects, music and narration.

Click on **Begin a new story** and then click on **Import Pictures** on the first screen. Choose about ten pictures from your school trip (it helps if they are all in the same folder on your computer). Click **OK** and the pictures will be imported into Photo Story.

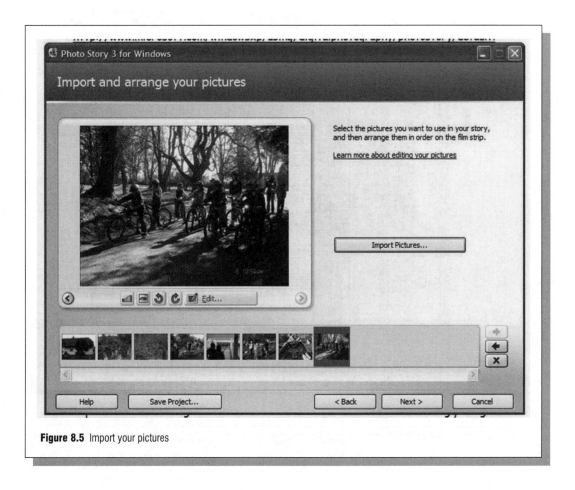

Figure 8.5 Import your pictures

You can change the order of the pictures, then add special effects and titles to each photo. When done, click **Next** and on the next screen you can customise motion, select transitions and narrate your story.

To narrate the story, click on the **Record** button and speak clearly into the microphone. When you click on the **Customize Motion** button, you are offered two tabs, one of which (**Motion and Duration**) allows you to state where you want the beginning and the end of the motion and also how long you want it to last. To see what the effects of these choices are, click on the **Preview** button at any time. The other tab (**Transition**) demonstrates a large variety of transitions you can choose from to move from one frame to the next one. Similarly, you can preview these to get the right one for your presentation.

When you are happy that the motion and transitions are right, go to the next page where you can choose a musical background. Click on the first photo in your timeline and then either click **Create Music** to create your own soundtrack from a selection of musical phrases or **Select Music** to select a soundtrack from your computer. If you are going to publish your Photo Story (say on YouTube or the school website) you should not choose background music, which is subject to copyright for reasons explained in Chapter 14.

Figure 8.6 Narrate and customise motion

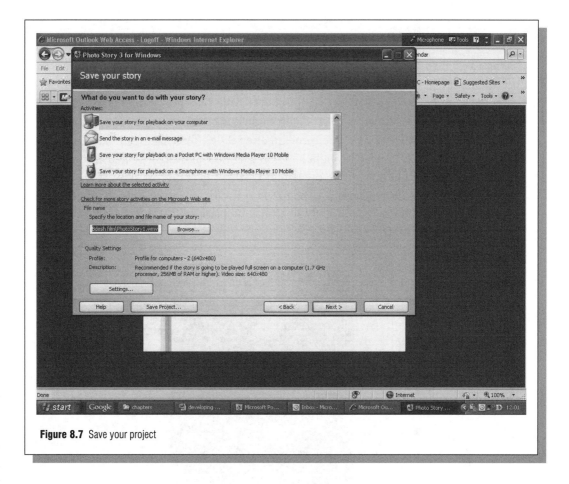

Figure 8.7 Save your project

Once you have selected the background music, **Preview** your photo story for the last time and click on **Next**. How you save your Photo Story depends on what you want to do with it. You can save it for playing back on your computer, for emailing as an attachment or for playing on a pocket device (like an iPod or a mobile phone), and the size of the file will vary accordingly. The best quality for playback is achieved if you save for playback on your computer. Save the project by clicking the **Save Project** button, and you will be able to go back and edit it. Then browse to where you want to save it (as a WMV file) and click **Next**. The photos, effects music, narration will all then be combined to make your Photo Story.

There are several websites that give you other ways of using your images: 280 Slides offers all the presentation tools of PowerPoint, but also offers the ability to share and display your content online, which can be ideal for those who do not have the software at home. Animoto makes 30-second movies with still photographs. Comicbrush allows you to make comic strips with your pictures. BigHugeLabs is a website that allows you to make calendars, collages, jigsaws, mosaics and lots of other fun things with your pictures.

Using video cameras

There are video cameras to suit children of all ages, and it is now possible to harness the power of the computer in the classroom to turn footage into professional looking films with fades, credits, soundtracks and effects. Many schools have handheld camcorders, but most digital cameras have a video function. You might find yourself supporting a class that is making films, but with a little expertise you could run an afterschool film-making club!

Flip video cameras are lightweight and compact, so can be easily taken around school or on trips. They have a flip out (hence the name) USB connection that allows for quick uploading onto a computer. Flip cameras have their own software, which allows easy sharing and mixing of films and the addition of music to create a presentation.

Figure 8.8 Flip video camera

Making movies can be great fun and involves a lot of different learning opportunities. There are the obvious ones, such as writing a script, as well as the less obvious ones, such as working out timings or framing the images. It can also be great for working with groups, as pupils can be allocated different roles and responsibilities, and they are collectively responsible for the outcome.

As well as a digital video camera, it is very useful to also have a tripod, an external microphone and a set of earphones. This is because, while it is very tempting to keep the camera moving and constantly zoom in and out, it is better to keep the camera still (hence the tripod) and make any changes in focus quite restrained. The external microphone will improve the sound quality and is a useful prop for interviews, and the headphones will tell the sound or camera crew whether the reporters or cast can be heard. The children will need to know how to use the equipment and be warned against trapping their fingers in the legs of the tripod! Whatever camera you are using, children need to be taught what constitutes a good film. By watching a few clips, perhaps from the television, they can learn about aspects of film such as lighting, sound quality and the camera angle necessary to get certain shots. Clips from the news make good source material as they convey information in quite a short time. Talk about the use of close ups, how long each clip lasts, voice-overs, and how the different reporters look at the camera or position themselves when interviewing people.

There are many different styles of film, including video diaries; interviews with expert; voxpops (unrehearsed interviews with members of the public); documentaries (about a school trip); or adverts, perhaps for the school. However, you could also use video for pupils to record what they are learning, such as creating a video in science about 'pneumatics', which will both reinforce their learning and show parents what they are doing in school.

Start quite small, as even a five-minute video could take more than an hour of filming to create. Whatever you are doing, there are several important roles to be filled when making a film, whatever age the children are. They will work in groups to do the research and then draw up the storyboard of shots. (Storyboards are very helpful: literally drawing the story like a comic strip to sequence the film and plan the shots.) They will have to think about the way the film will look; choose locations; and be aware of background sound and lighting.

You need a minimum of two people to do the filming. They must choose the correct background, angle of shot and lighting to get the desired effect. Somebody needs to make sure everything is heard and recorded clearly. The sound is very important, and filming must stop if something is not audible.

The editing software Windows Movie Maker comes with all Windows-based computers, and the highly regarded iMovie comes free with Apple Macintosh computers. There are also specialist titles such as Adobe Premiere Pro, Pinnacle Studio or Final Cut Pro, which are used by professional film makers. Whatever you use, they tend to work in similar ways. The screen will have three elements, a preview window, another window showing the video clips that have been downloaded from the camera and, at the bottom of the screen, a storyboard showing the clips in order with the effects and transitions showing. Having shot the film it should be a straightforward procedure to connect the camera to the computer with a firewire lead and let it automatically move the footage across. The film should show up on screen in the segments in which it was shot. When the camera is connected up to the computer, it is possible to record directly onto it.

Using Movie Maker

If you have been using an ordinary small digital camera in video mode, the process of using Movie Maker will be slightly different. The camera will show up as an extra drive on My Computer, and you will need to click on **Import Video** on the task bar of Movie Maker and then search for the relevant video clips.

Editing is reasonably straightforward, being simply a case of dragging and dropping clips into the timeline. Likewise, cutting clips can be done by pulling along the handles at the bottom of the preview window. Effects, transitions (such as fading between scenes) and titles (click on **View video effects**, **View video transitions** or **Make titles or credits**) are similarly dragged onto the storyboard from a window that replaces the clips.

Once you have completed your film, save it either to your computer for playback, to a CD, or as a smaller file that can be emailed. Some of these require you to save the film in different

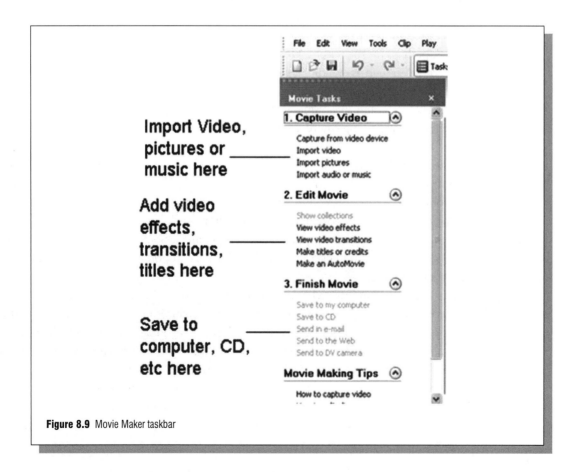

Figure 8.9 Movie Maker taskbar

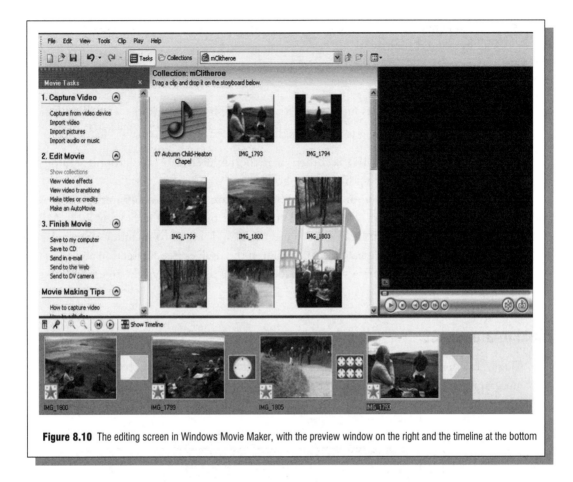

Figure 8.10 The editing screen in Windows Movie Maker, with the preview window on the right and the timeline at the bottom

formats. You can find out about how to do any of these by visiting the Apple or Microsoft websites, which have tutorials on using the software.

Teachers and children are using video to add another dimension to their presentations and assessments. Remember, when creating videos, good planning, clarity of purpose and clear roles and responsibilities all contribute to getting the best results.

Podcasting

Podcasting is an excellent way of allowing children to share their work and experiences with a large audience over the internet.

Children of all ages benefit from making them:

■ It allows children to develop and practise speaking and listening skills.

■ They develop literacy skills (writing scripts, setting up interviews, etc.).

■ They also learn important ICT skills.

- The audience can be invited to send their comments, giving valuable feedback to the children about their work.

- It gives them a potentially large audience for their work, including friends, parents and other family members.

- Children with difficulties such as dyslexia can publish their work in a way other than writing.

- It is great for developing teamwork skills.

You will either need an MP3 recorder (that the children can take around school for their interviews) or a computer with a microphone.

You will need podcasting or sound editing software on your computer, such as Audacity, which allows you to record your show as tracks, edit them and then export as an MP3 file to upload to your school website. You can use tracks and jingles to introduce particular features to the show – these can be created by the children themselves (see the section above on 'Making music') or downloaded from a website that allows the use of copyright-free music tracks, such as royaltyfreemusic.com.

Making a podcast

Begin by demonstrating some of the different radio genres, such as plays, information programmes, discussions and current affairs or news programmes. Then have a discussion about

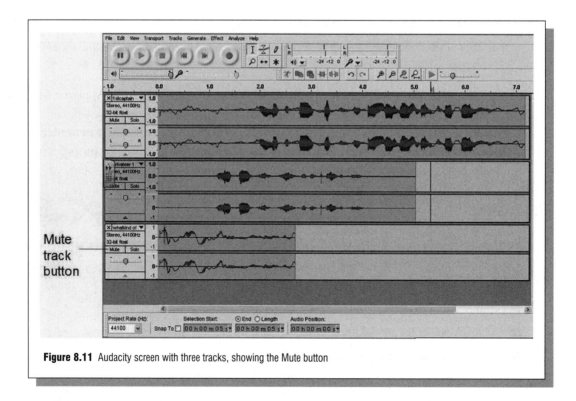

Figure 8.11 Audacity screen with three tracks, showing the Mute button

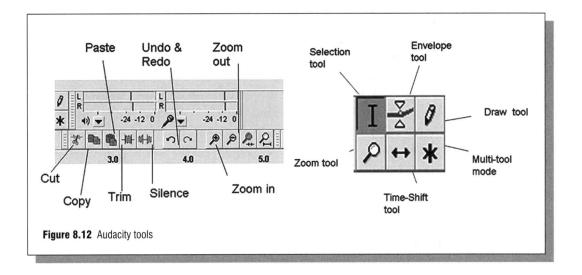

Figure 8.12 Audacity tools

what they would like to include in their podcasts. Children may want some music, some jokes, a quiz, a report, an interview; or they may be steered into making an article about Sir Francis Drake or the chickens hatching in the Reception class.

If they are recording tracks straight onto Audacity, connect a microphone to the computer. If they have recorded onto an MP3 player, connect them via the USB connector, then open Audacity and click **Project > Import Audio** (if you are using Version 1.2.6) or **File > Import > Audio** (with Version 1.3.10 beta) and navigate to where the files are saved. When you click open the file, it will be imported into Audacity.

Import any other tracks into Audacity, such as jingles, so that you have all the tracks you need for making your podcast. Listen to the tracks separately (mute the others by clicking the **Mute** button on the appropriate tracks) then use the **Silence** and **Trim** tools to edit them, and arrange them along the timeline, fading them in and out.

When the tracks are edited the whole project can be saved (**File > Save Project As**) and exported as a WAV file or an MP3 file (**File > Export As WAV file** or **File > Export As MP3**) for posting on the school website, or even uploading to iTunes.

Making stop-motion animated films

Children love to make animated films, and there are some good software titles available in schools to do this. Stop motion is an animation technique to make an object appear to move on its own. The object is moved in tiny increments between individually shot frames, creating the illusion of movement when the series of frames is played as a sequence. Many schools have Digital Blue PC Movie Creator and small, handheld Digital Blue Cameras.

If you are using the Digital Blue cameras, they sit in a small cradle and attach to the computer via a USB lead. To do a stop frame animation project the children need to decide what story they want to animate. This can range from the 'Hungry Caterpillar', to the story of 'Rama and Sita' for RE, to the story of Scott's expedition to the Antarctic or Mary Anning finding fossils on the coast at Lyme Regis. They then need to create their backgrounds on A3 paper and storyboard their shots and the action in each scene, identifying the characters and making them from card or modelling clay. Modelling clay is the most easily manipulated and clay figures will also stand unsupported. If using card, it may be easier to have your camera above the stage looking down (by attaching the camera to a clamp) and have the stage flat on the table or floor. When everything is ready, place the characters in position, open the software and start shooting.

There are three buttons on the left, and the top one is for shooting the film. Shoot your frames by clicking the **green camera button**. When you have at least five frames for each set, adjust the characters' positions a tiny bit; the smaller the adjustments the smoother the movements will seem on the film. When you have manipulated your characters and reached the end of a scene (or if you have made a mistake and think you might need to trim a clip), click the **red button** on the right and your pictures will be stored in the temporary folder in the stock (open the stock by clicking the **arrow button** at the top.) Your clips must be moved to the permanent stock otherwise they will be lost when the program is closed. Continue shooting all the scenes in your film and save all your sequences of shots.

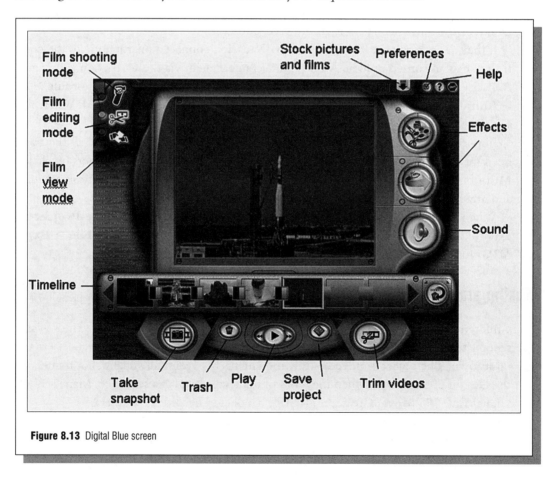

Figure 8.13 Digital Blue screen

When you are ready to edit the film, click the **middle button** on the top left and then click the **downwards pointing arrow** on the top right to open the stock. A timeline will have opened at the bottom of the screen. You can drag and drop your clips into the timeline. The **Trim Videos** button will put red sliders on the preview screen that will allow you to trim away sections. The two top buttons on the right will give you various special effects and allow you to put credits on the movie. Using too many special effects will detract from the main task of publishing a good movie, so decide whether you will allow the children to use them. The bottom button on the right allows you to add sound. There are some music tracks, special effects sounds and a microphone button for you to record your own voice (which needs to be done in a quiet room and carefully timed).

When all this is done, you should save your film and export it in AVI or WMV format, each of which should play on most media players.

Creating original works as outlined in this chapter – including music tracks, photos, videos, animations and podcasts – allows students to express themselves more creatively and gives them skills for life in the twenty-first century.

The opportunities of working online

There used to be a time when schools had to buy boxes of software for the 'multimedia' computers they had in classrooms. There are still some items of specialised software that need to be purchased, but so much of what we do on computers can be done online: from editing images; drawing pictures; doing tests; responding to surveys; joining discussions; word processing; mind mapping; translating phrases; searching dictionaries, thesauruses and encyclopaedias; sharing videos and commenting on them; posting statistics on weather stations and other scientific experiments; to managing the whole information systems for schools including pupil grades, attendance, reports and the SEN register.

You will find that all schools have some kind of management information system (MIS) and most schools have a managed learning environment (MLE).

Management information systems

A management information system is a computer system that manages the information that a company or organisation needs. Most schools have an MIS upon which is entered student details, plus records such as attendance, performance data and progress. They are valuable in enabling report writing, home–school links, assessments, target setting, budgeting and school self-evaluation. They offer support for the Head, Deputy and SENCO and for the administration officers or bursars in school.

The MIS will integrate with the school's MLE, so that everyone in the school community can access learning resources and school information.

Managed learning environments

MLEs are internet-based software systems that provide tools for learning and collaboration online. Many schools subscribe annually to an MLE. They support delivery of the curriculum

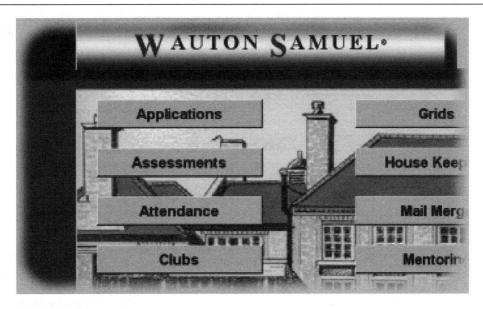

Figure 9.1 A page from a management information system

and tracking and assessment, and they aid communication. They also support collaboration between teaching staff and between students.

The tools of an MLE include: email, contacts, calendar, a portfolio, tools for blogging and online meetings, and tests and forums. Teachers can upload assignments where students hand in their work online, individually or as a group, so that the teacher can then correct, comment and assign grades. Some MLEs have tools for shared documents, sound recording, videoconferencing, podcasting and collaborative use of whiteboards. They can be used for demonstrating children's work to parents, who might log on with their child's login details at home (see Figure 9.2).

Working online: Using the internet

The internet began in the late 1950s as a way for the American military to send messages securely. The way it works has not changed: bits of information travelling across a network of computers; but the language the internet uses today, hypertext transfer protocol (the 'http' seen at the beginning of web addresses), was introduced in the early 1990s mainly as a way for academics to share their papers. Google estimates that in 2008 there were one trillion (as in 1,000,000,000,000) unique URLs on the web at once! There are two ways of finding what you want on the web, typing in an address or doing a search. Web addresses are sometimes referred to as URLs (uniform resource locators) and are typed into the address bar of the 'browser' (such as Internet Explorer, Firefox or Chrome).

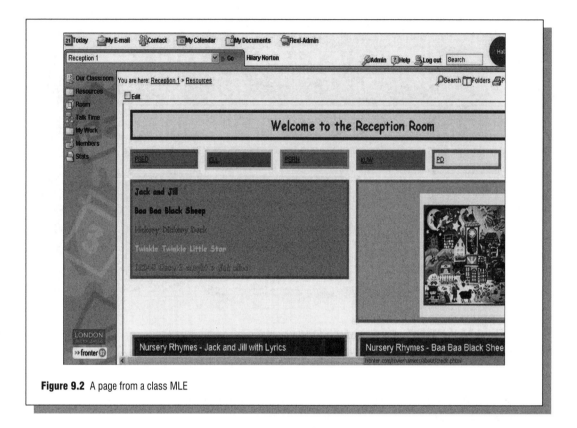

Figure 9.2 A page from a class MLE

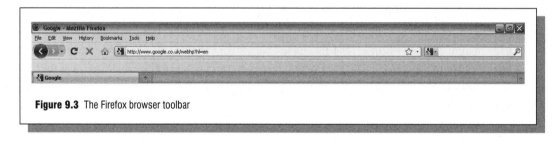

Figure 9.3 The Firefox browser toolbar

The address is made up of different segments, each of which mean something specific. Many addresses will begin with 'www' for World Wide Web followed by the 'domain name', the name the website owner has chosen. The last section tells you what type of site it is and what country it originates from, although American addresses do not bother with the country element. These additional elements are known as 'extensions'. Some common extensions are:

- .com – company (.co is the same thing but needs to be followed by a country extension)
- .gov – government
- .ac – post-school educational institution such as a university

- .sch – school

- .org – an organisation such as a charity

The country extensions include:

- .uk – United Kingdom

- .nz – New Zealand

- .au – Australia

- .fr – France

The different elements of an address combine to direct users to varying websites. For instance, adding different elements to 'www.canterbury' will take you to a variety of sites. So, www.canterbury.ac.uk is Christchurch College University of Canterbury, but replace the 'uk' with 'nz' – www.canterbury.ac.nz – and you get University of Canterbury in New Zealand. Similarly, www.canterbury.gov.uk is Canterbury City Council, but www.canterbury.nsw. gov.au is the local government of Canterbury in New South Wales, Australia. Other variations include www.canterbury.co.uk – a guide to Canterbury and surrounding areas and www. canterbury.net.nz/ – which provides web resources having to do with Canterbury in New Zealand. As you can see, accuracy is essential when typing in an address.

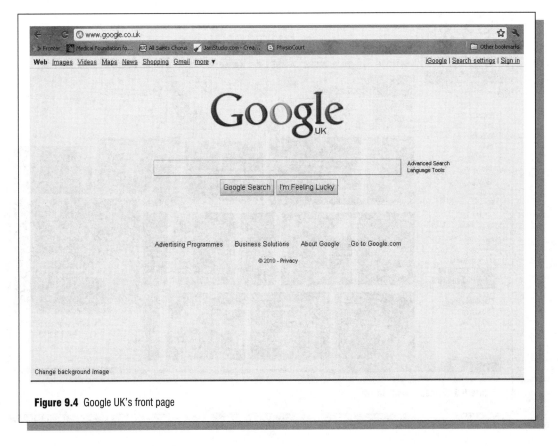

Figure 9.4 Google UK's front page

If you do not know the address of the site you want, or if you are using the internet for reference purposes, you will need to use a search engine. There are a number of these, such as Bing, Ask Jeeves, Yahoo, AltaVista and MSN; the most widely used, however, is Google, to be found at www.google.co.uk.

As you can see there are a number of options available when searching. Usually you will type in a word or words and then click **Google Search**. You could restrict the search to the UK, or use the **I'm Feeling Lucky** button, which will take you directly to the most popular page for that search term.

Another useful search tool is the 'Images' tab, which only searches for pictures. To get images for a project on space I might type in 'planets' and click **Google Search**.

This gives 'about 13,800,000 results (0.12 seconds)', or hits, as can be seen in the small print underneath the Google Search box. In order to narrow the search down I need to be more specific, perhaps looking for pictures of a particular planet. However, a search for 'planet Mars' will still bring over 3,270,000 results. Again, being more specific will help.

'Surface of Mars' brings about 1,700,000, but if I put the phrase in speech marks – "surface of Mars" – I get only 46,400. This is because Google looks for pages where the search terms

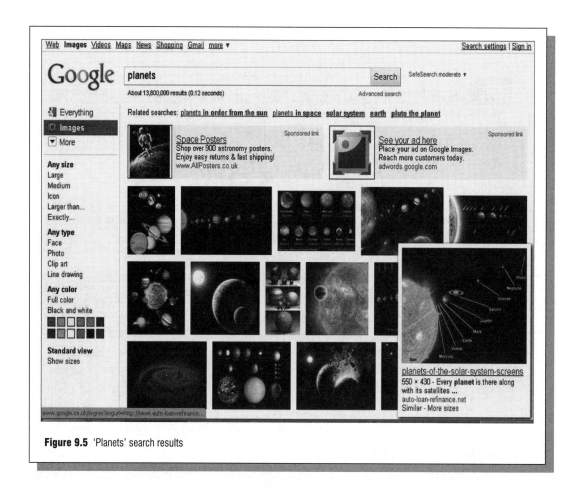

Figure 9.5 'Planets' search results

Figure 9.6 A picture of Mars copied from the NASA website where the copyright notice states, 'Photographs are not protected by copyright unless noted'

occur on the same page, not necessarily all together as a whole phrase. By putting them in speech marks it only gives results where the words appear next to each other. Adding more terms, such as 'NASA' will narrow the results down further – in this case to 28,400.

When finding images on the internet it is important to remember that, just like with printed material, they may be copyrighted (see Chapter 14).

To go to a page or image in the results list simply click on the link to go to it. (You will know if a link exists because the cursor changes to a finger, when you move over it.)

Once you have found an image you want to use, the easiest way to copy it is to point at it and **right click**, that is, click with the button on the right side of the mouse rather than the left. From here simply choose **Copy**, then open or go to the program you are copying into, such as Word or PowerPoint, then **right click** again, and choose **Paste.**

It is also possible to copy text from a website in a similar way, by first of all running the cursor over it to highlight it.

There is a large quantity of material on the internet, much of it unsuitable for school students. You can do a search yourself before the pupils so that you can guide them to suitable sites or help them refine their 'search terms'. You could save websites into the Favourites folder and instruct pupils to use only these sites. To do this visit the pages you want to include, then follow **Favourites > Add to Favourites**, give the page a name, or put it in a particular folder and then click **OK**.

You should also teach children to monitor the internet themselves and to report any inappropriate pages to an adult. Every school has an 'Internet Acceptable Use' policy, which will require staff, pupils and parents to sign a statement about using the web and specifying the sanctions for unacceptable usage. They should also be taught to think about the information they find and its validity, as well as the skills of questioning and discrimination.

Other ways to protect pupils when using the internet can found in Chapter 10.

Blogs and wikis

People all over the world are blogging. Blogs are about communicating. You observe your experience, reflect on it and then write about it. Other people read your reflections and respond by commenting or writing their own blog article. As well as text and web links, blogs can contain audio, music, images and video. Teachers have used blogs to facilitate 'peer review', meaning that students can post writings to the web, and other students can respond or encourage through the comment feature.

A class blog that posts questions about current subject matter can be a great way to introduce students to responding in writing and contributing collaboratively. For instance, a teacher might ask specific thought-provoking questions about a book the class is reading, and then ask students to respond through the comments feature with their ideas.

A wiki (from the Hawaiian word for 'quick') is a collaborative workspace, a website where a group of people can work together to create new content. It is built on a template that lets you decide the elements that are going to remain the same and lets you add pages and content simply. Wikis are often places where a small number of people are working collaboratively on a document. The most famous example of this is Wikipedia, a project where people from all over the world are working together to create a multilingual online encyclopaedia. The first person creating a wiki may upload an initial draft of a text. Subsequent visitors to the wiki can then read the original draft, comment on it, edit it and improve on it.

Year 7 children recently created a wiki about their school for the benefit of Year 6 children in a feeder primary school. All the children in the group of twelve took photographs, recorded videos and sound files as well as writing short pieces to introduce their school and loaded them onto wiki pages on the internet. These pages were then linked to from the school website so prospective students and their parents could get the pupils' perspective of the school.

There are many blogging sites – Blogger, WordPress, Typepad, – where you can start a blog. If your school is using an MLE, there will almost certainly be tools for blogging and collaborative work.

Social networks

We all know about Facebook and MySpace and other social networks. A social network usually has facilities for blogging, groups and forums. Each member has a page they can personalise

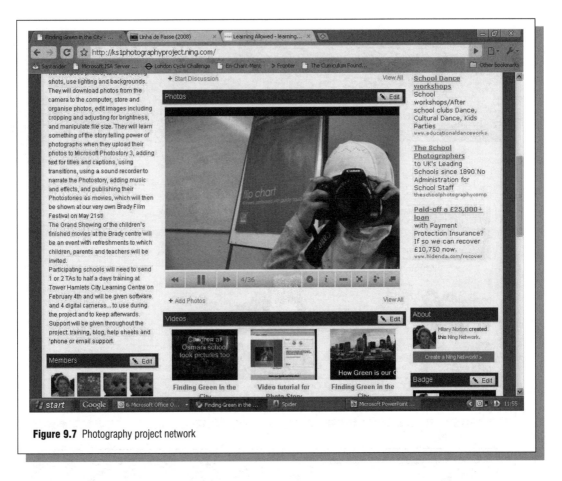

Figure 9.7 Photography project network

and a place where they can load photos and sometimes videos. Most youngsters will join one of these social networks – it's a place for gossiping to friends and identifying with certain groups.

It is possible to create a social network for one particular group of people, for example, for the duration of a project, like the one shown in Figure 9.7, for teachers and teaching assistants who were working together on an after-school photography project with KS1 children. Adults from about twenty schools came for training on photo editing and presentation software. The project took place over a term, and the teachers and teaching assistants had support from the trainer who attended some of the after-school clubs, but they also had recourse to a network on the internet specially set up for the project.

Members of the network were those who ran the project, those who attended the training and ran the clubs, and other interested parties such as head teachers or deputies. All the training help sheets were available on the network; training videos, example photographs and an example of the finished product; as well as a forum for questions and answers, an evaluation survey and a calendar with dates of training, clubs, deadlines and the Grand Photographic Show.

As well as being useful for adults to share professionally and socially, social networks can be useful in the same way for children. A social network created for a couple of KS2 classes can

Figure 9.8 Training videos

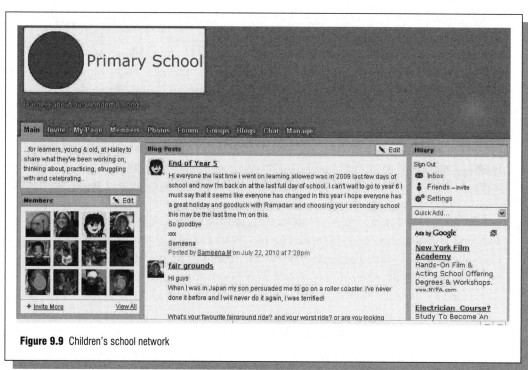

Figure 9.9 Children's school network

be a place for collaborating on work, sharing photos and more, developing all sorts of literacy skills and for learning how to stay safe, not to give away too much information about themselves and be in control. The classes can be in the same school or in separate schools in different parts of the country.

Many of the benefits of a social network can be achieved by using the school MLE, but having experience on a small scale can give teachers opportunities to teach children how to use larger social networks effectively and safely.

Online mapping

Most of us have been using online maps for years now. Common ones are Multimap, Streetfinder and Google Maps. They are great for those of us who get lost outside a three-mile radius of our homes, and now that they often include a satellite 'bird's eye' view or even a street view, it is possible to see exactly where your friend's house is in relation to the junction. You can search an online map to find out all the pizza restaurants near your home or to see a particular bus route. You can find the directions from your home to anywhere in steps and print out maps and directions.

Most of you will have played around with Google Earth if only to have put in your postcode and zoomed to hover over your house and see the washing out in next door's back garden. As well as being great fun just to play with, Google Earth and other maps are great for teaching too.

Here is a lesson about animal habitats that would be suitable for KS2 children, which teaches them:

- about the concept of a habitat and how they provide organisms found there with conditions for life

- how animals and plants have adapted to live in different habitats

- how to find images of different habitats around the world

- how to find information about these habitats and what lives there

- how to create an interactive map, using the example of animals in the Sahara desert.

First of all, make sure that Google SafeSearch is set to strict filtering. To do this, click on the **Preferences** link on the Google home page to the right of the search box or the **Search settings** link in the upper right corner, then click next to **Use strict filtering**. (There are several pages of help and guidance on Google to help you find your way around the tools: go to http://maps.google.com/support if you need them. The teacher will also need a Google account to use My Maps.)

Start by asking the pupils whether they can name some different habitats around the world. Using Google Earth or Google Maps on the interactive whiteboard, try to find some of the examples that they suggest – for example, the Sahara desert or the Brazilian rainforest.

Once this has been done take one example of a habitat, for example, the Sahara desert. Search in Google Images for 'desert animals'.

Figure 9.10 A Google map of the Sahara

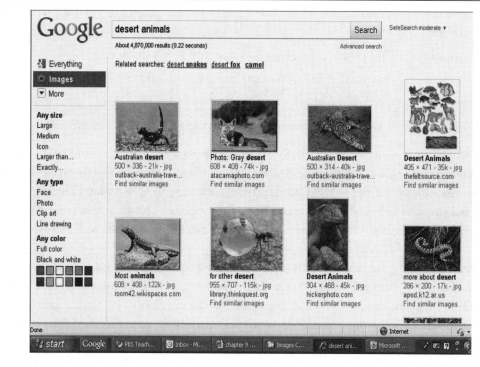

Figure 9.11 Google search for desert animals

Figure 9.12 Place marker on Google Maps with information about the camel

Introduce one or two animals that are specially adapted to live in deserts where the temperature is often very high and water is scarce. You could choose the camel, which can drink vast quantities of water in one go and uses its hump to store food for a long time, or a fennec fox, which has large ears, allowing heat loss to keep it cool.

Using Google Search, Images, Maps and Earth, pupils could work in teams to research and put together a presentation about a particular habitat. They could find animals that are well adapted to living in their chosen/assigned habitats. They could use Google Search to find information about how the animals survive in their specific habitats. They could add information to place-marks in Google Maps, showing where their habitat is, a picture of the animal from Google Images and a brief description of the special adaptations that allow them to live there.

Local mapping

It is possible to map events that are going to happen as well as stories and histories of an area. Records of what has happened in an area can be linked to specific places so that anyone can click on that link to find the history. It is possible to map ideas – or at least the places where

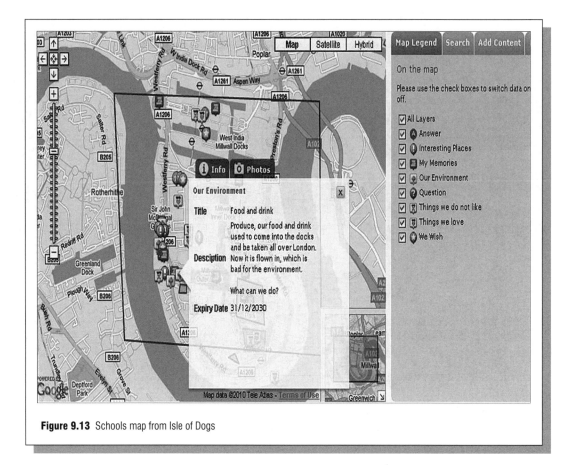

Figure 9.13 Schools map from Isle of Dogs

ideas can turn into reality: possible sites for growing food or creating new play spaces, or sites that are unsafe or polluted and need to change. The same maps can document positive transformations, social and environmental impacts and serve as a permanent archive.

As well as a project linking students from a school in the UK to a partner school in Senegal through the use of their own online interactive map, community mapping has worked with primary schools in inner cities to develop child-centred views of the local community and raise awareness of issues around sustainability.

Mapping for Change (www.mappingforchange.org.uk) is a social enterprise that supports the development of sustainable communities. It specialises in providing participatory mapping services to a variety of organisations, including schools.

Webcams

A webcam is a small camera connected to the computer that allows computer users elsewhere to see you clearly when using particular software. It works the other way round as well – a webcam situated in a zoo can give you a view of the zoo when you log on to the website hosting the webcam. If you have ever used the internet to find out about traffic conditions on the motorway or in the city, you will very likely be offered a website with a 'traffic cam' so you can actually see the state of the traffic. Many people use webcams and software such as Skype for keeping in touch with family in far-flung places. In schools, webcams have their place as well. The nursery class might have eggs hatching baby chickens or ducklings that they want to tell others about. A webcam can enable them to show other classes, even other schools. A webcam can be used when a child is off sick for a period of time and needs some contact with friends at school. This can take a bit of organising. However there are many webcams that are set up and running all the time that are great for 'taking' the children to the Serengeti National Park, Eileen Donan Castle on the road to Skye in Scotland, the Eiffel Tower in Paris and many other places across the world. Some webcam sites worth visiting are:

- www.bbc.co.uk/nature/animals/
- www.earthcamforkids.com
- www.bbc.co.uk/england/webcams/index.shtml
- Barnaby Bear (www.bbc.co.uk/schools/barnabybear/)

The Barnaby Bear website is a geography site aimed at KS1 children. It is based on the QCA Geography Scheme of Work 'Unit 5 – Where in the world is Barnaby Bear?'. Barnaby travels round the world introducing children to places at home and abroad.

The Barnaby Bear website contains games, videos, stories, a scrapbook and photo album and can be used independently or in association with the Barnaby Bear TV programmes. The games and activities on the site also complement work undertaken in other units, particularly 'Unit 1 – Around Our School', 'Unit 3 – An Island Home' and 'Unit 24 – Passport to the World'.

10

Being safe online

Internet safety is not a new problem, but it is a growing one, as we all – both children and adults – increase our online activities. The spread of the web, and access to it, means it is no longer enough to think about e-safety solely when pupils are in school, or at home. Nowadays, they could as easily be online in a library, a youth club or a cafe, or out and about on the bus, in the park or at a friend's, using a netbook, a phone, an iPod or a games console. The ubiquitous nature of internet access means that we need to make sure our response is similarly wide ranging.

Concerns

We are all aware of the ways in which 'stranger danger' has become an online concern. The ease with which we can connect to, and communicate with, others is one of the strengths of the web, but it is also one of the dangers. We cannot be sure that those we meet online are who they say they are. This makes it easy for those who prey on young people to hide behind the technology and get closer to them than they might in other situations.

However, the threat from strangers is less common than that posed by the increase in the forms of bullying that new technologies make possible – so-called 'cyber-bullying', which includes malicious text messages and emails, comments posted on notice boards and hurtful clips on YouTube, among other possibilities. Teaching staff, just like their students, are susceptible to this.

For adults, and older pupils, there is also the possibility of identity theft – thereby becoming the victim of fraud – or hijacked email accounts used to conduct malicious campaigns. And it is not just personal details that can be taken by others, so can creative works, such as coursework. Plagiarism (passing off someone else's work as your own) has increased exponentially since the advent of the internet as sharing work goes beyond a close circle to encompass anyone, anywhere studying the subject.

As well as other people's work, the internet can also be a source of misinformation. Anyone can post whatever they wish to online, so children can inadvertently be exposed to content that at the least is troubling, and at worst highly damaging: not just pornography but violent images, racist and sexist materials, and others that feed fears and prejudices around religion and beliefs, etc. While much of the inappropriate content will be automatically blocked by a network's filtering system, other less obvious material may slip through. Groups spreading racial hatred, for instance, may post very plausible sites denying the Holocaust, which children might take at face value.

There are a number of ways in which teaching assistants will be expected to help protect children from these concerns, and to respond to safeguarding issues that arise, following child protection procedures where necessary [STL 7.2 K7,11; STL 8 K20]. These include monitoring internet access and intervening 'promptly where actions may be dangerous' [STL 7.2 P5]. What those actions could be will probably be outlined in a school's ICT policy, the appropriate aspects of which you should know [STL 7 K10; STL 8 K1] including how to use any technological tools provided [STL 7.2 K12; STL 8 K19].

How to keep children safe online

There is plenty of information available on how we can protect our children when they are online, whether surfing the net, using social networking sites or texting on a mobile phone. A report by Dr Tanya Byron in 2008 examined children's use of the internet in detail and concluded that generally their usage was valuable, although the strengths and the weaknesses of going online were seen as closely aligned. The fact that information that supported learning was easily found is beneficial, but it was also easy to come across inappropriate content. Similarly, people can connect with others, for social purposes, to develop interests or to share information. But those others may not always be who they say they are.

In her report, Byron suggested three main ways to protect children. One was to provide age classifications on interactive materials such as video games. Another was to use technological methods such as filtering systems. The third, and most important, is to teach children to look after themselves when online. Technological approaches to e-safety and teaching children to look after themselves online are each discussed below.

Technological approaches to e-safety

Just about every school in the UK that is connected to the internet will have some sort of filtering system in place. There are essentially two approaches to this. One is known as the 'walled garden', which is where access is only allowed to a prescribed list of websites. Only if a site is on the list can anyone using the network look at it, although adding sites is usually a straightforward activity for teachers. The advantage of this method is that it is entirely safe as everything students get to see will have been vetted and approved by staff. The disadvantage is that the internet is a rich and ever growing resource, so much useful content will inevitably be inadvertently excluded.

The second approach is the more common one of filtering pages as users try to open them. These systems work by automatically scanning the content of websites and blocking them if certain rules are breached. These include bad language and pornographic content, sites that have no clear owner, others that do not control who can link to them, and those with suspect domain names. This method is by no means perfect. Undesirable pages will still slip through and useful, educational content will be barred. However, these systems also have reporting functions to alert the managers of the filtering process to know when an unsuitable site has evaded the filters and a request function to allow access to blocked sites.

When working with children online you need to know how to respond should a problem with accessing web pages arise, either because they are inappropriate, or they are unnecessarily blocked [STL 7.1 P7; STL 7.2 P5 and K6,9,10,12,16,23,24; STL 8.2 P11 and K10,18,19,27,29]. This can be as simple as clicking a link on the alert page requesting access to the contents, or sending a request to an ICT coordinator, technician or network manager.

Teaching children to look after themselves

A widely used analogy about online safety is that of the swimming pool. We can put a fence around one, with locks on the gate and lifeguards on patrol, but the best way to keep children safe in the water is to teach them to swim. So it is with e-safety.

The ICT curriculum will contain a number of elements to help pupils to stay safe online. Some of this will be directly focused on safety, talking about the possible risks and teaching children what to do to avoid them, and how to deal with problems that arise. Other areas that support e-safety include understanding how to evaluate the validity of information, and learning about managing pupils' own, and others', personal information.

When teaching children about keeping themselves safe online there are a number of practical steps they can be told to take. The degree to which they need to learn about each of these will vary depending upon their age, although children now join social networking sites from quite young ages. (Although Facebook, for instance, has a policy that only over-thirteens can join, there are no protocols in place to check the age of someone when they sign up.)

Children should be taught the following:

- Whenever they feel uncomfortable online, or they feel they do not have control of a situation, or they come across something that bothers them, they should tell an adult.

- They should protect their personal information and never give out their details, including phone number, email address, and home address online. They need to agree with friends that they will not give out each other's details, either.

- Passwords and PIN numbers should be used to prevent unwanted access to mobile phones, computers and handhelds. These should not be shared, even with friends.

- They should lock the computer if they leave it, and make sure they sign off when they finish, especially in public places such as cafes and libraries.

- When using forums and chat rooms online, young people should use a screen name, not their own name.

- They should only accept as friends online people they already know.

- They need to know how to use the privacy settings on social networking sites so that only people they want to contact them can do so.

- If they post photos or videos of themselves, or other people, they should think carefully about whether they might be embarrassing in the future. Friends should promise to do the same.

- If they ever meet someone in real life they have only known online, then they need to take a friend, or an adult, and tell people where they are going and when they will be back.

- If they receive abusive messages, whether text, email or on a social networking site, they should not delete them, as they can be traced back to the culprit. (It is useful to know how to take a screen shot using Print Screen for this purpose.) Similarly, they should know how to keep a copy of their online chat (by copying into a word processor, for example).

- They need to know about the 'Report Abuse' feature on websites, which connects either to the site's owners, or to the Child Exploitation and Online Protection (CEOP) centre – a national, multi-agency organisation.

- Older children should know that some online activities are criminal offences, including cyber-bullying, stalking and using someone else's details.

- They should be wary of using webcams and of other people online asking them to pose for photographs or videos.

One problem with internet use is that the more experienced young people become, and the more they understand how it works, the more inclined they can be to take risks, perhaps believing that they are able to control situations in which they may find themselves.

What schools can do

As well as providing children with the knowledge and understanding they need to keep themselves safe online, there are a number of other things schools can do create a safer environment.

All schools should have an acceptable use policy (AUP) in place. This lays out what anybody – both adults and children – using the school network can, and cannot, do when on it. Typically it will include types of websites that are proscribed, guidance on the downloading and uploading of files, a requirement to check for viruses and requirements to be respectful in communications.

These AUPs are often sent out at the beginning of the school year for parents and pupils to sign as part of the behaviour contract. Reminders are often included as part of the sign-on routine in schools, so that anyone wishing to use the network has a prompt to accept the conditions before they can start working.

While it is hoped that staff would not need to sign such a policy, that their professional approach to their work would be enough to ensure appropriate conduct, this is, unfortunately, not always the case. For inexplicable reasons, people online do not apply the same levels of restrained and courteous behaviour as they might when meeting face to face, or when not working virtually.

Because of this, many places have adopted protocols for staff when using social networking sites, as well as AUPs. Such requirements might include that they do not 'friend' pupils. Or if they have a need to connect through such media, that they create a professional, online, profile. In this way items such as photos from private gatherings will remain out of reach of the children. Although such protocols often also suggest that it is best not to post any photos that you do not mind being widely seen – not only in case pupils, and parents, come across them, but also because potential employers might have a look online at any applicants. This can result in them finding additional skills not mentioned on the application form – although they could also find, for instance, photos from a hen night in Blackpool.

Another part of the home–school agreement can be permission to publish photos of children. Once such permission was simply to cover inclusion in spreads in the local paper. Now it covers schools creating their own newsletters, and more importantly, putting images online. This can be important for a number reasons. One is that adults wishing to contact vulnerable children might identify them from images then track them down at the school.

Most schools have their own website, which usually contains a gallery of work and records of recent events. When uploading these, schools need to be careful of providing too much information. Other precautions can include only using school-based email addresses for staff and pupils, so that restrictions can easily be put in place, or messages traced.

Working with parents

As well as involving parents in helping children to stay safe online in school, a wider e-safety strategy will also help to keep them safe at home. This could include events to raise parental awareness of how young people use the internet, what the possible risks are and what can be done to minimise these.

Guidance to parents might include information on:

- using filtering software, which often comes as part of anti-virus software or in a broadband package
- keeping computers in family rooms, so they can always see what children are doing
- agreeing time spent online for work, and for socialising
- talking about cyber-bullying and what to do about it
- being careful who children accept as friends, and accompanying them if they want to meet an online friend somewhere
- making sure that their children understand how important it is to keep their details private – and their parents' details too

- being aware of places outside the home that children can get online and checking to see that these are also active in keeping children safe online.

Safeguarding procedures

In principle, responding to an online incident is no different from how you would deal with any other safeguarding concern. Online safeguarding is about child protection, not ICT.

- You will need to listen to the child and reassure them that they are not at fault, telling them that you will respect their right for information to be kept confidential, but that sometimes the law requires you to pass it on.

- Any evidence to do with the incident needs to be preserved. With online materials this could include taking screenshots and compiling them into a document, copying message threads into a word processor and saving web pages.

- The designated teacher for child protection (usually a senior manager) needs to be made aware of the incident. They will decide what to do next.

- Keep it confidential. Only pass on details to people who need to know.

Overall, being online benefits lives, providing access to rich resources, a range of media, and many ways to learn and to connect with other people. Given the amount of time we spend online, and the number of other people doing the same thing, the risks of a child coming to significant harm are low. They are also very real. In helping children to live safe, confident, online lives it is important to retain a balance between the positive impact these technologies are having on our lives and the risks that are associated with them.

11

Taking control – putting yourself in charge

Always remember who is boss when using technology – even when you are not sure what you are doing it is still you who has the finger on the off button. There are times when devices do inexplicable things – crashing, freezing, connecting to the internet, ignoring basic commands, lining up text in the wrong place and refusing to move it. The document you have spent half your life creating (well, a couple of hours anyway) suddenly disappears from the screen. Some of this is beyond our control – we just have to accept that these things happen – but a lot of the time we have more power than we think.

There are two things you need to know: who to ask for help, and a bit of basic IT first aid. At school, the first of these may be a technician, ICT coordinator, class teacher, fellow teaching assistant or even a knowledgeable pupil – it depends what you want to know and how big the problem is. Checking that everything is working and knowing how to report problems is required for the knowledge section of the NVQ [STL 7.1 P6,8,9; STL 7.2 P6,8 and K5; STL 8.2 P11 and K27]. You also need to make the computer, or other equipment, safe, either by marking it so people know not to use it, or even by turning it off.

Troubleshooting

Check the power

If a piece of ICT equipment, whether it's a computer, a printer, a mouse or a video player, refuses to work, the first thing to do is to check that all the leads are pushed in firmly and that the electric socket is turned on. For instance, when the printer will not print, check it has power and that both ends of the printer lead are correctly in place. If you are happy that this is the case and it still will not work, isolate it (pull the plug out) and call the technician.

Correcting mistakes

Just as with learning to drive, the first thing to do on a computer is to learn how to stop when things start to go in the wrong direction.

If you have made a mistake while using a piece of software you can usually put things right with the **Undo** button. You can also undo by following **Edit > Undo** or, simplest and quickest, holding down **Ctrl + Z**.

There are also times when software starts to do something that you do not want it to do. On a web page you can simply click the **Stop** button. Other times you either have to let it load then close it or go back, or you can try pressing the **Esc** button at the top left of the keyboard. This will sometimes interrupt whatever is happening. However, the main tool in regaining control of your machine once it begins to get out of hand is to hold down **Ctrl + Alt + Del** together, which opens the Task Manager. This will show you a list of all the programs running, often including one that has 'Stopped responding'. Click on this program and then on the **End Task** button to close whatever has stopped. Take it easy when you press **Ctrl + Alt + Del**, though, as doing it twice may restart, or reboot, your computer.

Rebooting the computer

Many problems with computers, and other devices, will resolve themselves by rebooting the machine. If a computer has stopped responding – to the degree that even **Ctrl + Alt + Del** will not work – rebooting can be achieved by holding down the power button until the machine goes off (sometimes more than 10 seconds will elapse). If you have to resort to this, you may lose some work, although it is likely that the program will have an auto recovery function that will automatically show you the document you were working on when it crashed, once you get going again. You can then open it and carry on. Something might have been lost, but usually only the last five minutes worth, not the last five hours.

Setting up equipment

There may be occasions when you are responsible for setting up and operating equipment, such as a laptop, moveable interactive whiteboard, a peripheral such as an iPod dock, or even a CCTV camera for a child with a visual impairment. This will often be because a teacher has asked you to, so you need to confirm the requirements [STL 7.1 P1] and check the resources are available [STL 7.1 P2].

Setting up ICT equipment is seldom complicated, although you should refer to any instructions provided while doing so [STL 7.1 P3]. Many connections have become standardised, in particular the universal serial bus (USB) connections. Other leads are designed to go into only one place (often referred to as a 'port') and so are almost impossible to connect incorrectly. If you have to force any connector into place then it is probably not the correct port. If a USB lead will not plug in, try turning the connector up the other way and gently push it in again.

When setting up, you need to ensure that the 'learning environment meets relevant health, safety, security, and access requirements' [STL 8.2 P1].

Installing software

There may be rare occasions when you need to install, or re-install, software. You will need to talk with your technical support first, as this usually requires administrator rights of access to the computer's operating system. However, sometimes there may be a need to install a particular piece of software for a pupil, or an activity downloaded from the internet, that will not cause problems on the network. Or you might be working with a child who has their own laptop, a standalone machine, so there is no need for a high-level technician to be involved. Normally an 'installation wizard' will pop up to walk you through the process, and it becomes a case of simply clicking **Next** or **I Agree** to the licensing conditions.

General maintenance

Generally, as computer installations in schools become more complex it is best to leave it to those whose job it is to do these things. However, there are some jobs that might fall to anyone, such as replacing the ink and topping up the paper on the printer, or burning CDs or copying files to USB memory sticks to record work. These are reasonably straightforward and mainly commonsense tasks – you may want to be shown the first time, but after that it is the kind of thing teaching assistants frequently do in classrooms [STL 7.1 P4; STL 7.2 P7 and K4]. It is even the kind of thing that some of the pupils can do.

What to do if you think a machine might have a virus

All school systems should be protected by virus checkers. They usually run constantly in the background, which means that when you start up the computer they run a quick scan; they then scan any file you open, whether from the hard drive, a file server, a USB memory stick or an online file storage facility. They also scan webpages when you open them from the internet, as well as incoming emails [STL 7 K10].

If you suspect there is a virus on a computer, first of all report it to the ICT coordinator or technician. If you have the privileges, run a virus check by double-clicking on the anti-virus software and letting it check the hard drive. The scan should start automatically and, depending on the number of files scanned, quickly report back on how many files have been checked, whether viruses have been found and if it has solved the problem by deleting or quarantining these.

Organising files

One thing it is helpful to know is how to organise files on a computer system. The most useful analogy is to think of the computer as an office. The desktop is just that and the filing system is the filing cabinet: its drawers, hanging files and folders. And just like that system, it is possible to move things around between them, albeit in an electronic, virtual kind of way.

You may have heard of the hard drive – the permanent memory – in your computer being referred to as the 'C' drive. Other drives have different letters. Essentially all of these represent a place to store files – like the drawers in a filing cabinet. Fortunately the computer will be set up so that there is one common place that we will usually use and we do not have to hunt about each time to find the right drive. However, there are times when we might want to save a file elsewhere, on a USB memory stick, perhaps, to take home or to move to a computer that is not on the network.

Ordinarily when you click on **Save As** in the **File** menu, or click the **Save** button on the menu bar, the computer will open a dialog box to put the file in a particular place, which can be changed through the 'Save in' box to a different location, either on the network or on a portable device.

You can also move files around between folders, and between drives, both through these dialog boxes and through Windows Explorer. When using Windows Explorer you simply click on a folder to open it and show the folders and files it contains. Again, if it were a filing cabinet you would open the correct drawer, then the folder within it, then the file within that.

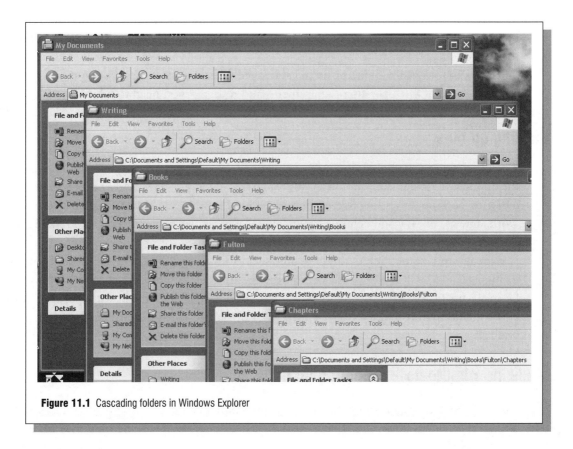

Figure 11.1 Cascading folders in Windows Explorer

As you organise your files, so you will create folders within folders. In this example, you can see this chapter is saved in a folder called, 'Chapters', which is itself in one called 'Fulton', which is in one called 'Books', within 'Writing', which is contained in 'My Documents'. This sequence is known as the file path and can be seen in the address bar of each folder. The document is located at 'C:\My Documents\Writing\Books\Fulton\Chapters'. To move the document to another folder, I could either use the 'Edit' menu and **Cut** it and **Paste** it into another folder or use 'drag and drop' to slide it across the screen. If the new location is on the same drive, it will be moved; if it is on another drive, 'G' – a USB memory stick – for instance, it will be copied.

You can use these same techniques for adding files from external devices. Photos from a memory card, for example, can be copied across to your 'My Photos' folder without having to open them in editing software and using 'Save As' to move them.

When working with pupils you may need to make sure each has their own folder and that their work is saved into it. Primary school networks are often set up with a folder for each class to save work into. At secondary level, students are likely to have their own username and password to log on to the computers, so work is saved automatically into their own space, their network area.

Increasingly, file management is moving online, either through using space provided by internet companies – Microsoft has SkyDrive – or on a school's learning platform. This works in much the same way as saving files on the network, the difference being that the place the file resides is not physically on the school premises, but somewhere on a server elsewhere in the world.

(Knowing the details of logging on, what is saved where, and how files can be shared between users are some of the 'operating requirements and routines' you need to know for STL 7 K6.)

Backing up files

The other thing you should do is save regularly and back up files, and you should encourage the pupils to do likewise, so should a catastrophe strike you will have a recent copy somewhere, either to be immediately recovered or to be found quite easily. Most programs save as you work anyway, but it is still helpful to develop good habits, such as clicking on the **Save** button every so often, or pressing **Ctrl + S**, which is the keyboard shortcut for saving.

Backing up is something that few people seem to do very often, the exception being ICT technicians who will regularly back up all the files on the network, often nightly. This might be an automatic, external backup to a secure server offsite, or they might use a portable device.

It is useful to know what system is used in case you ever need to retrieve files for pupils, or yourself.

Knowing what to do – becoming intuitive

The difference between computer users who are confident and those who are not is who they blame when things go wrong. The uncertain will assume that it is something they have done.

The confident user will blame the machine or the software. Sometimes things might go wrong because of something they have done, but they will either see this as a temporary blip until they have learned how the software works, or will simply find a way around the problem.

So the first thing to do to in becoming an intuitive computer user is to change your attitude. It is not you who is at fault, you can do these things, it is the machine and the way it works that is getting in the way of success.

The second thing is to find what is common between programs. Almost all programs have menu bars, the words that sit at the top of the screen. And quite often the commands within those menus will be the same across all programs. So within the 'File' menu will be the 'Save' command. There will also be a 'Save As' command so you can change the name or type of a file, or keep an earlier version than the one you are working on. The next menu across will almost certainly be the 'Edit' menu where the 'Cut', 'Copy', and 'Paste', commands are located. The last menu will be the 'Help' menu (also found in most programs by pressing the **F1** key).

The more you use programs the more you will notice the similarities between them. For example, the 'Active Object' – the one you are working with whether it is a picture, a chart or a text box – will have black or white dots on the corners and sides, its handles. These can be used to resize it, by holding down the mouse button and dragging. Or it can be moved when the double-headed cross style of cursor appears. You will begin to expect these things and to work with them naturally.

Watch the cursor change to see what sort of action you can take. Is it the browser finger for a link, or an arrow to select an object? Take notice of the screen: what is it that changes when you take certain actions? When you get a pop-up box to give you information, read it even when you do not know what it means. It might one day make sense.

Finally, ask how something is done. Confident people see others using programs and they want to know how they did what they just did. Users who are comfortable with computers are not uncomfortable about not knowing. They realise that no individual can know it all, so they exchange tips all the time. Not knowing is not a problem, not asking is.

Talk the talk

You also need to sound like a skilled user. It is important when working with pupils that, as far as possible, you use the correct language. In part this is so that you and they are clear about the learning that is happening as words provide the framework on which to hang the concepts they have learned. These words allow them to talk about the subject accurately and are a useful tool for assessment [STL 8.1 P8 and K26]. If the language of the subject is used correctly, it is a clear indication learning has taken place.

When working with the pupils, explicitly teach the language of the subject. Every scheme of work should include key vocabulary. When using spreadsheets this might include, 'cell', 'model', 'formula' and 'reference'. Ask the pupils for definitions and then explain the additional meanings. For example, as well as being a place to keep prisoners, a 'cell' is also part of a living organism and, more crucially, one of the spaces on a spreadsheet. An 'address' is where you live as well as where you will find a particular web page. In this case you could also use the term 'URL' – it is a more accurate term that older pupils should understand even if they do not use it often.

If you are not sure what the key vocabulary is, you should ask the class teacher, or you could look it up. Most schools work with schemes of work issued by the QCA. These can be found on the internet at the QCA website (www.qca.org.uk). Even if a school is not using these schemes, the schemes will still give some idea of the language of the topic. These can be put on posters on the wall and given out to learn as spellings for homework.

For example, here is some of the vocabulary children might encounter in Year 3:

- database
- field
- record
- file
- sort
- classify
- order
- bar
- chart
- simulation.

When they get to Year 7 they will also need to know:

- address
- cell reference
- value
- variable.

Some computer terms are difficult to define – 'value' for instance, again from spreadsheet work. If this is the case, look it up. While it might mean how much we will pay for something, it is, according to *Webster's New World Dictionary of Computer Terms*, 'A number entered into a spreadsheet cell'.

To be a confident and competent computer user, act like one, talk like one and, as you get to know it better, develop a greater understanding of what the computer really can do – and a healthy scepticism about much of what it is claimed it will do.

12

What is good ICT teaching?

There are occasions when your work with pupils might come under particular scrutiny. One is when Ofsted comes visiting. Another is during your assessment for the NVQ.

Like it or not, the judge of what constitutes a good school in this country is Ofsted. What Ofsted wants to see is both good teaching of ICT and good use of ICT in teaching and learning across the curriculum. So what does it look for?

What Ofsted wants to see

For a start, Ofsted looks at the entire educational provision within a school, which includes lessons, lunchtimes, after-school clubs and teaching assistants. It is unlikely that an inspector would observe you directly and comment on your work. What they are most interested in is how you work within the classroom. How you work with the class teacher to deliver the curriculum, and how what you do with groups or individuals fits in with the learning intentions of the lesson. This is as true in ICT as in every other subject.

Most of what an inspector will look for is common sense and likely to be how you work anyway. They will want to see that teachers have some idea of what pupils already know; how the lesson they observe fits into the broader scheme of work; that the learning intentions are clear and are known by the pupils; how well the pupils engage with the learning; and that there are opportunities built in to the lesson to check that learning is happening.

Planning for the lesson

The lesson needs to be well planned and clearly structured, although this does not mean that if a fruitful learning opportunity offers itself this cannot be pursued. Your role should be clear – who you are working with, what resources you will be using and how you will be working – if this is not the case do clarify it with the class teacher [STL 8.1 P2,4,6; STL 8.2 P2 and K2,4,5], particularly as it is the sort of thing an inspector might ask about. If you are supporting a particular group of students, or even an individual child, then the learning objectives for them need to be clear, and known by you, as will the criteria for assessment [STL 8.1 P8].

You also need to know just what the lesson will consist of, what you will be directly teaching and what resources will be used. It is quite possible that the lesson is based on the scheme of work developed by the QCA, as this provides a good benchmark for the curriculum. If it is not, then the school needs to show that the work pupils are doing is just as challenging and rigorous and that the National Curriculum is being sufficiently well delivered.

The inspectors will also be looking to see how well the pupils work with the ICT resources, both in the subject area and in other lessons. Are they confident? Do they have a positive approach? Are their skills appropriate to their age group?

While typing up a smart copy of an essay from their work books to the computer can produce a room full of young people quietly tapping away and engaged in the task, it is not necessarily good ICT teaching. If all they are doing is transferring the text from one medium to another and the exercise is merely to provide smart copies to stick on the wall, you have to wonder what is wrong with their handwriting? If, on the other hand, they are working from notes or a plan, developing their work as they go and using formatting features, such as changing font attributes or adding clipart, then they are exploiting the benefits of using a computer.

If you do find an inspector in your classroom be sure you know what the aims of the lesson are and what the learning intentions are for any particular pupils with whom you are working. Also be sure that you are comfortable with using the technology and talking to your charges about it.

NVQ observation

Observation is a good way to cover many of the Performance Indicators in both Unit 7 – Support the use of information and communication technology for teaching and learning, and Unit 8 – Use information and communication technology to support pupils' learning.

NVQ Level 2

The assessor might observe you talking to the teacher before the lesson, to confirm the resources to be used [STL 7.1 P1], set them up [STL 7.1 P3], check they are working [STL 7.1 P6] and inform the teacher of any problems [STL 7.1 P2,8], while making sure any equipment that is faulty is safe [STL 7.1 P9]. If you check that the resources are suitable for the children [STL 7.1 P5], that consumables (ink, paper, batteries) are available [STL 7.1 P4] and that the internet filtering is working [STL 7.1 P7], then all the PIs for this element will have been covered.

The criteria for STL 7.2 shift the focus towards supporting children in learning, although STL 7.2 P6 and P7 seem to repeat PIs from 7.1. They also add a requirement to make sure equipment is left safe and stored properly [STL 7.2 P8,9]. While working with the children you will need to show that you can operate the resources correctly [STL 7.2 P1], instruct and support the pupils [STL 7.2 P2,3] and provide 'an appropriate level of assistance' to help them to 'experience a sense of achievement' [STL 7.2 P4]. You will also need to make sure the children are safe, both in the way they use equipment and online [STL 7.2 P5].

The Knowledge evidence for STL 7, denoted by a K, can also be assessed by observation. Again, there are some repetitions, such as making sure equipment is available [K3], knowing where the consumables are [K4], knowing how to report faults [K5] and making sure things are put away securely [K25]. Other criteria can be assessed through how you work with the children, demonstrating your knowledge of the programs they use [K13,14,15] and how to help develop ICT skills and develop independence [K17,19,20,21,22].

NVQ Level 3

Even when you move up a level, the need to ensure your work is coordinated with the class teacher remains key. In STL 8.1 you need to show that you talk to the teacher about the 'opportunities for using ICT to support pupils learning' [P1], to ensure resources are appropriate [P2] and to agree on procedures for assessment [P8]. In STL 8.2 there is more scope for your teaching skills to shine.

Here you will show your use of ICT in learning activities with pupils, ensuring that it is integrated [P2]; pupils are engaged in learning [P3,10]; they have time to explore [P4]; they have equality of access [P7]; and they are making progress [P9]. As they work you will encourage them to use the resources available effectively [P6] and to work with elements of the ICT curriculum, such as solving problems and finding new information [P5]. All the time you will help to ensure that the materials match their preferred way of learning [P8], and you will respond to problems that arise [P11]. After the lesson, you will help to feed back on how it went for them [P12].

In order to do all this, quite a lot of your background knowledge could emerge. For example, you might support pupils in particular ways and use particular methods of teaching and learning [P22,23], or maybe adapt the ICT resources for the pupils [P11,12], or use them to support pupils with SEN [P14]. Quite naturally, you will probably allow them time to explore the ICT [P24] and show high expectations of their learning [P15].

Your knowledge of assessment will also be evident here and how you find out what progress they have made in learning [K16], which could happen in other curriculum areas [P21].

What an observer might look for

When observing an NVQ candidate, there are some things that are done, or avoided, that demonstrate an ability to help children to learn ICT skills. These are some of them:

- Feedback is frequently given, even just a passing comment that the correct button has been clicked [STL 7.2 P4].

- Praise is focused on effort and achievement; it is not given just for the sake of it [STL 7.2 P4].

■ Questions are focused on the task. They support learning, asking the children to explain what they are doing or how they worked something out [STL 7 K21; STL 8.2 P3,6 and K16,24].

■ The TA seldom touches the equipment, the mouse or keyboard, directing the pupil rather than doing it for them [STL 7.2 P2,3 and K13; STL 8 K15].

■ Clear instructions are given based on a sound knowledge of the programs and an understanding of the learning intentions behind the task [STL 7.2 P2 and K13,14].

■ Sometimes the TA holds back from intervening, or answering a question straightaway, allowing children to solve problems for themselves [STL 7.2 P3,4 and K17,20,21,22; STL 8.2 P3,4,5 and K15,24].

■ Children can help each other, although they should not take over – showing others what to do, not doing it for them [STL 7 K21,22; STL 8.2 P5].

■ If the pupils drift off task, or misbehave, the focus is on getting them back to work, not on the undesired behaviour [STL 7.2 P3,4; STL 8.2 P11].

■ All children, not just the dominant ones, get to answer questions, to have a go at a task and to show off their work. This may require extra effort to ensure particular groups, girls, perhaps, or pupils with special educational needs, are engaged and involved [STL 7 K18,19; STL 8.2 P7,8,9 and K25,26].

■ Different ways to learn and to demonstrate what has been learned are explored. This will include finished products, talking about what is happening, demonstrations and teaching each other [STL 7 K1,15; STL 8 K22,23].

■ The appropriate vocabulary for the task is used by both staff and pupils [STL 7 K21; STL 8.2 P12].

■ Children are encouraged to give each other feedback, through appropriate, supportive discussions [STL 7 K21,22; STL 8.2 P12].

■ Adaptations are made to the task, the resources or the assessment to help the pupil achieve the expected learning outcomes [STL 7 K18,19; STL 8.1 P7,8,10 and K12,14].

■ Task-focused feedback is provided to the teacher and the children [STL 8.2 P12 and K16].

Observation should be for your benefit

Any sort of observation, whether by an anonymous Ofsted inspector who slips into the room for a brief period, or by an NVQ assessor who you have got to know quite well and whose judgement you trust, will be stressful. However, with the NVQ any observation will be discussed with you in advance to make clear what Performance Indicators and background knowledge it is expected will be observed. Often additional evidence arises, and observations can be used across a number of units, so an ICT lesson could also see you Promote Positive Behaviour [STL 19]. If the expected evidence does not emerge, then another observation can be arranged. It is a process designed to provide you with an opportunity to demonstrate your skills, rather than make a snap judgement about your capabilities.

13

Health and safety issues

Despite the fact that we come across them everywhere and use them all the time, computers can be bad for your health, although those at risk are mainly people who use them all day, every day because they are an integral part of their work. In schools this is not yet the case. Problems identified include physical ones, such as repetitive strain injury (RSI) or backache, eye strain and headaches. Much of the risk can be removed or reduced by setting up our working space properly, taking breaks and doing exercises.

Although school staff and pupils may be at less risk than others, adopting some of these practices will make working with a computer easier and reduce any associated discomfort. You should ensure that both you and the pupils use computers safely [STL 7.1 P6,9; STL 7.2 P1,5 and K8,9,23,24; STL 8.2 P1 and K18] and that after use they are left safe and secure [STL 7.2 P8,9 and K25].

Computer workstations in schools are generally for multiple users, so they will not always suit everybody; however, some generalisations can be made, and where possible the setup should be flexible.

Key points for working at the computer:

- The user should be able to sit at the computer with their feet flat on the floor, with their knees lower than their buttocks.

- The forearm should be at the same height as the keyboard, so that when typing it is either parallel to the floor or sloping slightly downward.

- Wrists should be held up, and flat or curved slightly downwards. A wrist rest can be used to achieve this. Hands should not bend upwards from the wrist.

- There should be about a hand's width between the keyboard and the edge of the desk.

- The top of the monitor should be level with or slightly below eye level and able to be tilted by the user for comfort. It should be about 35 cm to 70 cm from the user.

- There should be enough space to put working documents beside the machine.

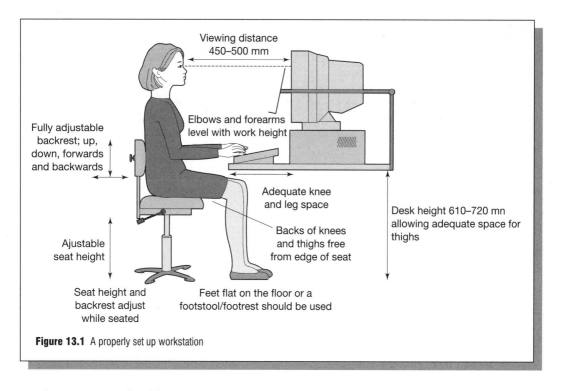

Viewing distance
450–500 mm

Fully adjustable
backrest; up,
down, forwards
and backwards

Elbows and forearms
level with work height

Adequate knee
and leg space

Desk height 610–720 mn
allowing adequate space for
thighs

Backs of knees
and thighs free
from edge of seat

Ajustable
seat height

Seat height and
backrest adjust
while seated

Feet flat on the floor or a
footstool/footrest should be used

Figure 13.1 A properly set up workstation

The computer should be placed in a position where there is no reflection on the screen, although changing the angle of the monitor can usually solve this.

Computer suites, designed for the purpose, are often better set up than classroom computers, which are sometimes placed where their is a bit of unused space or a socket is available, rather than where the risks of discomfort are minimised.

Positioning computers in the classroom

Computers in classrooms can take up a lot of space, and the furniture used, even specially designed pieces, does not always allow for this. Ideally, chairs should be adjustable with no arms and the type of back that supports the lumbar region. Using higher chairs and providing footrests for small children will lift them up. Often the monitor is placed on top of the hard drive, which could be moved to the side or to a shelf on the wall. Space can be created by moving the printer to another place and buying a longer printer lead. Glare can be reduced by re-positioning the computer or even creating a screen-hood from sugar paper.

Laptops are often used at desks. As this is usually for shorter periods, having them well set up is less critical; however, children do still need space, and this may require some jiggling of desks and chairs.

Apart from promoting good posture while sitting at the computer, other good practice would include taking regular breaks (five minutes every hour as a general guide) and developing good keyboard skills. Touch typing and using keyboard shortcuts can both reduce strain on the limbs.

As mentioned previously, keyboard shortcuts allow you to use commands through the keys rather than the mouse, such as cut (Ctrl + X), copy (Ctrl + C), paste (Ctrl + V), print (Ctrl + P) or save (Ctrl + S).

Should anything breakdown or become damaged, you need to know what to do about it. Your priority must be the safety of the children and your colleagues. Your school will have health and safety procedures for you to follow. These will include commonsense instructions such as to turn equipment off and disconnect it from the mains. You may want to warn other users by labelling faulty equipment, or even prevent them from using it by removing the mains lead [STL 7.1 P8,9; STL 7.2 P6].

When you are sure the equipment can be safely left, you will need to report the fault. Most schools will have a system of reporting things in writing, although this can sometimes just be a word with the responsible person during break. However, try to keep a written record as this allows you to keep track of what has happened and what has been done about it.

There are some tasks, such as changing the bulb in the overhead projector or changing the printer cartridge, that you might want to do yourself [STL 7.1 P3,4]; however, for more complex problems, it is generally best to leave things to those whose job this is.

14

Legal knowledge

It goes without saying that in your use of ICT in the classroom you at all times act responsibly, both as a model to the pupils and to protect yourself from possible disciplinary action. While this will generally be underpinned by your common sense and your professionalism, there are policies and legislation that help to frame the parameters of your work.

One thing that you should have read and understood is the school's ICT policy [STL 8 K1]. This will help define what is acceptable and what is not, and outline your role when using ICT with pupils. It may also highlight specific legal requirements relevant to the school, particularly to do with online safety (see Chapter 10), data protection, copyright and licensing. These provide an important framework for working in schools.

While you will need to know little specific detail of any legislation, you will need to understand the general principles and how they have an impact upon your work [STL 7 K7; STL 8 K13].

Data Protection Act

You will need to bear this act in mind in the course of your work, although you will not need to quote it. Just be aware of the basic principles.

The Data Protection Act covers all instances when data is collected. It has eight principles, which say that data must be:

- fairly and lawfully processed
- processed for limited purposes
- adequate, relevant and not excessive
- accurate
- not kept longer than necessary
- processed in accordance with the data subject's rights

- secure

- not transferred to countries without adequate protection.

In the classroom you will probably be handling data for two purposes:

- maintaining pupil records

- curriculum work.

In the first of these tasks you might be contributing to the record of pupils' achievements in school. This could be through discussion with class teachers, through keeping records of groups you are responsible for or through contributions, in writing or at meetings, on pupil progress. This latter might include annual reports or reviews for pupils with special educational needs.

In curriculum work you may be collecting information for data-handling. This could take many forms, but might include personal pupil information, from such things as shoe size to number of people in the family or distance they live from school.

The application of the Data Protection Act principles is largely a matter of common sense and will contribute to good practice in schools. When thinking about pupil records it means that comments or notes you make should be fair, based on fact and kept for a reason. They should be dated and attributed – that is, it should be clear who has made the record and when.

When working on classroom tasks with pupils, consider what information can be shared. Pupils may be sensitive about certain information, but this is more about good practice than data protection.

Overall, data protection is about common sense and individual rights to privacy and fairness. Your school should have a member of staff designated to deal with data protection issues, usually a member of the senior management team, so any thing you are not sure of can be dealt with by them.

Copyright

Copyright is intended to make sure that an individual's efforts are not exploited by others through unauthorised use. It broadly covers anything that is created and published, whether it is a book, a song, an image, a computer program or a website and is meant to ensure that any earnings go to the creator, along with the due acknowledgement of their work and ideas.

This does not mean that every time you use someone else's work you have to ask their permission. Generally schools are covered by the Copyright Licence Agreement (CLA), which allows for limited copying for specific purposes.

For paper publications this can be relatively easily specified. For instance, it could mean that a short story can be photocopied for a class to use, although no more than one copy per pupil, plus one for the teacher and support staff; or no more than 5 per cent of a complete book. However, electronic publications are more difficult to police, particularly websites that might cover several pages, have contributions from many people, and consist of several types of media, including text, music, images and video.

Schools also need to be aware of copyright law when posting content on websites. Logos, for instance, will be copyrighted, and while it is unlikely that a pupil expressing support for a particular football club by displaying their badge on a webpage would be prosecuted, this would be a technical breach of copyright. By creating and posting a webpage, the pupil will have re-published someone else's creative work.

The flip side of this is that intellectual property from a school's site, its name, a logo, or piece of work, could similarly be copied and re-published on another webpage, thus breaching the school's own copyright, or the student's right to be recognised as the creator. If you do publish something online that was not created within the school, it is best practice to acknowledge where it came from and to provide a link to that original place.

Much of the file sharing on the internet is illegal, and students should be taught that this is the case, that it is theft and that they risk prosecution if they are found out. In recognition of the openness of the internet, new types of copyright licence have come into being, under the general heading of Creative Commons. This recognises that creations posted on the internet are easy to copy and use as the basis for further work, so they set conditions that allow this to happen – but only as long as certain conditions are met, such as always specifying where the work originated.

Determining whether a breach of copyright has occurred can be a difficult thing. However, if you approach it with a view to respecting other people's work and acknowledge what has come from other sources – and what those sources are – and act in good faith, you shouldn't manage to go too far wrong.

Licensing

We often talk about licences for computer software. Whether it is installed on the computer, run from the network or downloaded from the internet, most of what we use will have conditions attached to its use. The licence specifies what those conditions are.

This is because when you use software, ownership of the program remains with the copyright holder. You have the right to use it in particular ways, laid down by the owner, but you do not really own it. Typically a licence will specify how the program can be used and the number of users or computers the software can be run on.

Types of licence

There are many different variations of licences. These are some of the common ones found in schools.

■ A 'single user' licence means the program can be installed and run on only one machine. To run it on more machines will require more licences, one per installation.

■ A 'site licence' allows it to be used on any machine on a given site, a geographical location. Strictly speaking a split site school would need two site licences, and if it is installed on laptops that travel to homes these should have more licences.

- A 'network licence' allows for the use of the program across a network of connected computers, so machines not connected to the network are not covered.

- A 'concurrent licence' lets the software be installed on any number of machines, although only a given number of users can run it at any one time. So if the licence is for ten users and an eleventh person tries to use the program, it will not run.

- 'Open source' software can be used without a licence. It has been created to share, and it is expected that if people develop it further they will also share it for free. Often it is covered by a Creative Commons copyright agreement (see above).

In practice, the programs you use in the classroom will be licensed when they are purchased, and either the ICT coordinator or a member of the senior management team will ensure that the terms of any agreements are adhered to.

Licensing agreements are important to protect the rights of the copyright owner to their intellectual property and to any income derived from it. It is also important for schools because institutions that are in breach of licensing agreements can be heavily fined, and individuals found to be illegally copying or using software can be disciplined and even dismissed. As well as protecting the network, this is one of the reasons that schools have clear policies and procedures on who can procure and install programs [STL 8 K9], including restricting the people who are allowed to do it.

It is unlikely that you will ever have legal difficulties when using ICT in school. If you are not sure, check with someone who should know. If in doubt, don't.

15

Keeping up to date and getting qualified

The NVQ fits within a framework – a continuum – of qualifications. You may have undertaken some training before starting work, and you might want to progress further once you have finished it.

Pre-NVQ

Teaching assistant professional development can now begin even before a TA enters a school. Courses are available, such as 'An introduction to support work in schools', both to help with preparation for the role and to improve chances of employment. There are then courses that support the development of the role, such as a Department for Education induction course.

Post-NVQ

The NVQ is part of the National Qualifications framework. At Level 2 it is equivalent to GCSE, and at Level 3 it is equivalent to A Level. For many teaching assistants, achieving the NVQ will be sufficient recognition of their professional capabilities. Others may wish to proceed further, perhaps to Qualified Teacher status.

Moving on to Level 4, which is equivalent to the first year of a degree course, can see teaching assistants becoming Higher Level teaching assistants. Beyond this is the achievement of a Foundation degree, which is a vocationally based qualification equivalent to the first two years of a Bachelor's degree. These require a greater level of reflection and a deeper understanding than the NVQ.

To go on to become a qualified teacher would require either taking a Bachelor's degree in Education, which would involve teaching practice in schools as part of the degree, or taking a degree in an appropriate subject and then doing a Post-Graduate Certificate in Education (PGCE). However, there are now other routes, such as Teach First or the Graduate Teacher Programme, where training is provided on the job while actually working in schools.

What else is there?

As part of the NVQ you are expected to think about how you can keep your knowledge up to date [STL 7 K26; STL 8 K30]. You can do this in a variety of ways – while attending training sessions is an obvious one, you can also teach yourself new skills, follow developments in the press or online, watch appropriate shows on TV and attend exhibitions.

However, you might also decide to follow other interests. Given the diversity of roles in schools, and the range of requirements, there are many other routes to take. In areas such as special educational needs, TAs are often developing specialisms, such as working with speech and language disorders or with children on the autistic spectrum, which can make them an authority in these areas. Other options include becoming a cover supervisor or an exam invigilator, or focusing on bilingual pupils. All of these have their own National Occupational Standards.

Appendix 1: National Occupational Standards for Supporting Teaching and Learning in Schools

STL 7 – Support the use of information and communication technology for teaching and learning

7.1 Prepare ICT resources for use in teaching and learning

Performance criteria

You need to:

P1   confirm the requirements for ICT resources with the teacher

P2   check the availability of the required ICT resources and promptly inform the teacher of any problems with obtaining the resources needed

P3   follow the manufacturers' and safety instructions for setting up ICT resources

P4   make sure that there is ready access to accessories, consumables and information needed to use ICT resources effectively

P5   confirm that the ICT equipment and software are appropriate for the pupils

P6   check that the equipment is switched on, ready and safe for use when needed

P7   check and maintain screening devices to prevent access to unsuitable material via the internet when appropriate

P8   promptly report any faults with ICT resources to both the teacher and the person responsible for arranging maintenance or repair

P9   ensure that any faulty equipment is isolated from any power source, appropriately labelled and made safe and secure.

7.2 Support the use of ICT resources for teaching and learning

Performance criteria

You need to:

P1   operate ICT resources correctly and safely when asked to do so

P2   give clear guidance and instructions on the use of ICT resources by others

P3   give support as needed to help pupils develop skills in the use of ICT

P4   provide an appropriate level of assistance to enable pupils to experience a sense of achievement, maintain self-confidence and encourage self-help skills in the use of ICT

P5   monitor the safe use of ICT resources, including internet access, and intervene promptly where actions may be dangerous

P6   regularly check that equipment is working properly and promptly report any faults to the appropriate person

P7   use only approved accessories and consumables

P8   make sure that ICT resources are left in a safe condition after use

P9   make sure that ICT resources are stored safely and securely after use.

Knowledge and understanding

You need to know and understand:

K1   the potential learning benefits of using ICT in different ways to support learning

K2   the sorts of ICT resources available within the school and where they are kept

K3   school procedures for booking or allocating ICT resources for use in the classroom

K4   the location and use of accessories, consumables and instructions/information texts

K5   who to report equipment faults and problems to and the procedures for doing this

K6   operating requirements and routines for different ICT resources with which you work

K7   relevant legislation, regulations and guidance in relation to the use of ICT, e.g. copyright, data protection, software licensing, child protection

K8   the importance of health, safety, security and access

K9   the specific requirements to ensure the learning environment is accessible and safe for pupils using ICT resources

K10 the school policy for use of ICT in the classroom including virus controls and access to the internet

K11 safeguarding issues for pupils who access the internet

K12 how to use screening devices to prevent access to unsuitable material via the internet

K13 how to provide clear instructions and guidance on the use of ICT resources

K14 how to use the software and learning programmes used by the pupils with whom you work

K15 how to select and use learning packages to match the age and development levels of the pupils with whom you work

K16 useful online and offline resources that support appropriate use of ICT

K17 the range of ICT skills needed by pupils and what can be expected from the age group with which you work

K18 how to adapt the use of ICT for pupils of different ages, gender, needs and abilities

K19 the types of support pupils may need to use ICT effectively and how to provide this support

K20 the importance of pupils having time to explore and become familiar with ICT activities and equipment

K21 how to support the development of ICT skills in pupils

K22 how to promote independence in the use of ICT resources by pupils

K23 risks associated with ICT resources and how to minimise them

K24 the sorts of problems that might occur when supporting pupils using ICT and how to deal with these

K25 school requirements and procedures for storage and security of ICT resources

K26 as ICT is a rapidly developing and changing area, how you will keep up to date in order to ensure you provide the best support and opportunities for pupils' learning through ICT.

STL 8 – Use information and communication technology to support pupils' learning

8.1 Prepare for using ICT to support pupils' learning

Performance criteria

You need to:

P1   identify and agree with the teacher the opportunities for using ICT to support pupils' learning within the overall teaching programme

P2   discuss and agree with the teacher the criteria for ICT resources to ensure the appropriateness for all pupils with whom you work

P3   explore and evaluate available ICT resources and consider how these can be integrated into the planned teaching and learning programme

P4   plan to use ICT to support learning in ways that are stimulating and enjoyable for pupils, according to their age, needs and abilities

P5   identify sources of ICT materials which meet the needs of the pupils and the teaching and learning programme

P6   ensure a range of ICT materials are available which meet the needs of all pupils including those with learning difficulties, bilingual pupils and gifted and talented pupils

P7   adapt ICT materials as necessary to meet the needs of the learning objectives and pupils' age, interests and abilities within copyright and licence agreements

P8   discuss and agree with the teacher how pupils' progress will be assessed and recorded.

8.2 Support pupils' learning through ICT

Performance criteria

You need to:

P1   ensure the learning environment meets relevant health, safety, security and access requirements

P2   integrate ICT into learning activities, providing the required adult support

P3   engage pupils in ICT activities by providing interesting and stimulating opportunities and challenges

P4   allow pupils time to explore and become familiar with ICT activities and equipment

P5   encourage pupils to use ICT to solve problems, work collaboratively and find out new information

P6   support pupils to use ICT materials and resources effectively to advance their learning

P7   ensure that all the pupils have equality of access to ICT provision, encouraging those who may be reluctant to participate

P8   monitor how pupils are responding to ICT programmes and materials to ensure that the programmes and material match the pupils' abilities and learning styles

P9   monitor pupil participation and progress and make judgements about how well pupils are participating in activities and the progress they are making

P10   modify teaching and/or learning methods, if necessary, to ensure pupils continue to be engaged and included in, and benefit from, planned activities

P11 take appropriate action to resolve any problems in supporting pupils using ICT

P12 evaluate and provide feedback to relevant people on:

    a)   pupils' participation and progress

    b)   the effectiveness of ICT in supporting pupils' learning

    c)   the effectiveness of ICT programmes and materials in meeting learning objectives for pupils with a diverse range of needs and abilities.

Knowledge and understanding

You need to know and understand:

K1 the school's ICT policy

K2 the potential learning benefits of using ICT in different ways to support learning

K3 how good quality ICT provision promotes pupils' physical, creative, social and emotional and communication development alongside their thinking and learning

K4 the relevant school curriculum and age-related expectations of pupils in the subject/curriculum area and age range of the pupils with whom you are working

K5 the contribution that ICT can make to meeting the planned teaching and learning objectives

K6 ways of selecting good quality ICT resources that encourage positive learning for pupils by applying selection criteria, eg. allows the pupil to be in control, has more than one solution, not violent or stereotyped, stimulates pupils' interests

K7 the range of ICT materials from different sources

K8 how to identify the benefits of ICT materials and sources of information and advice

K9 the school's policy and procedures for obtaining, adapting and using ICT programmes and materials

K10 the school's ethical code and/or equality of opportunities policies to ensure the suitability of ICT programmes and materials obtained

K11 how to adapt the use of ICT for pupils of different ages, gender, needs and abilities

K12 tools and techniques for adapting ICT programmes and materials

K13 the need to comply with copyright and licensing agreements for different ICT materials

K14 how to use ICT to advance pupils' learning, including those with special educational needs or additional support needs, bilingual pupils and gifted and talented pupils

K15 the importance of having high expectations of pupils and how this is demonstrated through your practice

K16 strategies for gathering information on pupil learning and progress through ICT, and how to plan for and use these in teaching and learning activities

K17 the importance of health, safety, security and access

K18 the specific requirements to ensure the learning environment is accessible and safe for pupils using ICT resources

K19 how to use screening devices to prevent access to unsuitable material via the internet

K20 safeguarding issues for pupils who access the internet

K21 how pupils use ICT as a tool to support learning in many curriculum areas and in doing this what they learn about ICT as a subject in its own right

K22 how to select and use appropriate teaching and learning methods to develop pupils' ICT skills and enhance subject teaching and learning

K23 the types of support pupils may need to use ICT effectively and how to provide this support

K24 the importance of pupils having time to explore and become familiar with ICT activities and equipment

K25 how ICT can be used to assist implementation of equality of opportunity, inclusion and widening participation policy and practice

K26 how to monitor and promote pupil participation and progress in learning through ICT

K27 the sorts of problems that might occur when supporting pupils using ICT and how to deal with these

K28 how to evaluate the effectiveness and suitability of ICT resources and materials for promoting pupils' learning

K29 useful online and offline resources that support appropriate use of ICT

K30 as ICT is a rapidly developing and changing area how you will keep up to date in order to ensure you provide the best support and opportunities for pupils' learning through ICT.

(Training and Development Agency for Schools, October 2010, available at www.tda.gov.uk/support-staff/developing-progressing/ nos/supporting-teaching-and-learning-in-schools.aspx)

Appendix 2: NVQ for TAs

Disclaimer – matching the criterion of the NVQ units to tasks is not an exact science. The PI and KB are given as indications of activities that could provide opportunities to show that they have been met. It is likely that in some tasks more criteria will be met than those listed here, and, equally, some will not be demonstrated and supplementary evidence will be needed. The majority of the criterion are covered at least twice in the suggested assessment plan below.

NVQ FOR TAS

ACTIVITY	CONTENT COVERED	STL 7			STL 8			IDEAS FOR RESOURCES
		7.1	7.2	KB	8.1	8.2	KB	
Answer the following questions: a) How does the school keep users safe when using computers, including protecting children when online? How is the school network kept secure? How are ICT resources kept safe? What is the procedure for acquiring new ICT resources? What do they take into account when deciding what to buy? How does the school make sure it meets legal requirements, such as copyright, data protection and software licensing? b) Get a copy of your school's ICT policy and list all the activities that you have some responsibility for. What do you do in class to put these into practice?	You need to show that you understand how the school keeps users, and equipment, safe and legal. This will include: • Filtering • Safeguarding procedures • Anti-virus software • Security procedures • Licensing • Copyright • Data protection. Who decides what ICT resources to buy? How do they decide? Who do they talk to? Who makes requests? By reading the ICT policy (and other policies that may be relevant, such as child protection) and highlighting areas that come under your role you should understand what your contribution to its implementation is. Write in the first person, e.g. 'I only use software provided and never download from the internet without authorisation.'	7, 8, 9, 11, 12, 25	5, 8	7, 8, 10			1, 9, 10, 13, 17	Some of the policies that may affect your work: • ICT and the Acceptable use Policy • Teaching and Learning • Safeguarding • Some websites will help with information, such as the Information Commission (www.ico.gov.uk), Becta (www.becta.org.uk), CEOPs (www.thinkuknow.com) and Wikipedia.
Provide two lesson plans, one for an ICT lesson, one for another subject where ICT was used. Write a learning log showing what you did in the lesson.	Include: The discussion with the teacher to clarify your role. What you did, e.g. 'Supported a small	1, 5	3, 18, 19, 24	9, 2, 8, 10	1, 7, 9, 12	5, 5, 11	2, 5, 11, 12	Think about how you followed the lesson, but how you might have changed the

ACTIVITY	CONTENT COVERED	PI/KB (ALWAYS READ THEM BEFORE COMPLETING A TASK)		IDEAS FOR RESOURCES
		STL 7	STL 8	
		7.1 7.2 KB	8.1 8.2 KB	
	group. Circulated the class to help as necessary. Targeted particular pupils. Say who you worked with, and whether you had to modify the learning aims for them. How? What difficulties were they having? How was the lesson assessed? How did the teacher know if the learning aims were met? How did this vary for some pupils? What feedback did you give the pupils you worked with? How? What feedback did you give the teacher? How?	11, 14, 12 15, 16, 21, 22, 25, 26		resources used. What prompts you might have given. What evidence there was to show the learning that had taken place.
Create a concept map of the ways in which ICT supports learning.	You might have branches headed 'communication', 'collaboration', 'creativity', 'access', 'learning styles', etc. Then from these have sub-headings, e.g. Communication – between pupils, between staff, between home and school, with other schools.	1		2, 3, 8, 25 ICT helps in many ways. They may not all be in use in your school, for instance videoconferencing can connect schools across the world, but your school may not be doing that. Include the potential uses as well as the actual ones.

NVQ FOR TAS *continued . . .*

ACTIVITY	CONTENT COVERED	PI/KB (ALWAYS READ THEM BEFORE COMPLETING A TASK)				IDEAS FOR RESOURCES
		STL 7		STL 8		
		7.1	7.2 KB	8.1	8.2 KB	
Make a table of the different sorts of ICT hardware in the school that you can use with pupils. Give examples of how they are used in learning; show how they are kept secure, what booking procedures there are, and where manuals and consumables for them are kept.	This is to show you understand the breadth of resources that come under the heading ICT, including computers, toys, cameras, digital recorders and so on. You might use column headings such as: Equipment Use, Security Arrangements, Booking Procedures, Consumables, Instructions. E.g. 'Digital cameras used in Y4 for recording a trip to the farm. Kept in the ICTCO cupboard, booked out with her. Requires batteries from the cupboard, memory cards with each class.' 'Toy till used in nursery in the role-play area. Left out all the time.'	4 7, 9	2, 3, 4, 25			You do not have to make a list of everything in the school, just the things that you could potentially use with the children.
Think of a subject that is due to be taught in your class soon, perhaps chosen from the medium-term planning. Make a list of all the ICT resources available to use to teach it. Beside each, explain the benefits or disadvantages of its use. Show which ones you would use, and explain why you have chosen them, and also explain why you think others are unsuitable.	It will help to look at the scheme of work and planning documents for this subject. Think about the range of learning needs of the pupils in your class, and issues such as ethnicity and gender, and look for ICT resources that best meet those needs. As well as the equipment in the school and the software on the network, think about CDs and DVDs that might have useful content.	2, 15, 16	3, 5, 6	6, 7, 8, 28, 29		It is important to be able to decide what will work with your pupils and what will not. Deciding not to use something can show as much about your ability to judge as deciding what you will use. Include resources for

ACTIVITY	CONTENT COVERED	PI/KB (ALWAYS READ THEM BEFORE COMPLETING A TASK)		IDEAS FOR RESOURCES
		STL 7	STL 8	
		7.1 7.2 KB	8.1 8.2 KB	
	Search the internet for resources and list some of those that you find, explaining which are suitable and which not. As an example, a geography lesson on erosion might include a MS PowerPoint, a digital camera to take photos, Google Earth to find images, the BBC weather website. Some pupils may need supportive software to help them make a record, such as a text predictor, or a grid of key vocabulary for writing it up.			particular children, such as specialist hardware or software.
Create an interactive, multimedia resource to use with a pupil, or group of them. Write about: • The learning aims you were meeting. • How this resource met the learning needs of your target audience. • Whether is worked as you expected. If you were going to use it again, what would you change about it? What would you do differently when using it?	This could be a presentation to use with a group, or something that individuals or groups use with or without adult support. The commentary should explain why this resource meets the learning objectives for this group, or why it does not. It does not matter if it has not worked as you wanted. If it did not meet the learning needs, showing that you understand why that is is just as valuable to demonstrate you know how to match learning resources to needs as if it was successful. It is your reflection on the resource that is important.	14, 7 3, 22 7	2, 4, 12, 14, 26	This could be anything that you create. Something for the whiteboard, a template for writing, an animation to explain how the knee works. You could use any appropriate software – PowerPoint, Smart Notebook, Flash, Word, Excel, iMovie, etc.

ACTIVITY	CONTENT COVERED	PI/KB (ALWAYS READ THEM BEFORE COMPLETING A TASK)		IDEAS FOR RESOURCES
		STL 7	STL 8	
		7.1 7.2 KB	8.1 8.2 KB	
E-safety – What does the school do to keep children safe on line?	Describe what the school does with regard to e-safety, including: • acceptable use policies • filtering • ICT lessons • dealing with incidents that arise • reporting child protection incidents. Include an outline of what needs to be reported to whom, and how concerns are escalated.	7 5 7, 8, 9, 10, 11, 12, 22, 23, 24	1, 11 17, 18, 19, 20, 27	It will help to look at the ICT scheme of work to understand how e-safety is taught to pupils. Some useful sources of information include www.thinkuknow.com, www.ceop.gov.uk, www.kidsafe.co.uk.
Use a piece of a pupil's work to show how ICT supported them in completing it.	This could be as simple as using a word processor instead of handwriting, or as complex as using a special computer set up (such as a touch screen or symbol package). You could also include how you help the pupil to use the computer, maybe supporting their hand on the mouse, or prompting their actions. For some children, this may be how you give praise and feedback.	3, 3, 14, 4, 5, 4 15, 5, 17, 6, 18 7	2, 3, 22, 3, 4 23, 4, 6, 24 7, 8, 12	This need not be complicated, for some children just using a word processor helps them to structure their work, to take it in stages, and to get round messy presentation. Others might use very specialist hardware or software.

ACTIVITY	CONTENT COVERED	PI/KB (ALWAYS READ THEM BEFORE COMPLETING A TASK)						IDEAS FOR RESOURCES
		STL 7			STL 8			
		7.1	7.2	KB	8.1	8.2	KB	
Make a visual record of a learning environment. Use this to comment on how well it is set up. What changes could be made. And who you would expect to make them.	You could use a photo, diagram or video. This could be the ICT suite, library or classroom (or all of these). Think about who is meant to use the area, what they will use it for, and whether the equipment is properly set up for them. Is there enough space for books and notes? Is the furniture at the right height? Can it be adjusted? What about the lighting or any noise? Could users be at harm, from hurting their backs or getting repetitive strain injuries (RSI)?	8	5, 6, 8	8, 9, 23, 24	1		17, 18, 27	There are lots of places on the web that show how computers should be safely set up. The Health and Safety Executive has guidance at www.hse.gov.uk/ pubns/indg36.pdf. Schools also need to think about anyone, including parents and governors, who might need to use ICT, perhaps as part of an evening class. Remember to include these people if necessary.
Assessment – Use a piece of pupil work to demonstrate your role in the assessment process	Describe the learning objectives agreed with the teacher. Show how the work meets these. Describe how you report pupil achievement to the teacher and how this is recorded.	1, 2, 8	9, 12	16				The lesson plan usually includes the range of levels pupils might achieve. You may also be reporting on what a pupil has

ACTIVITY	CONTENT COVERED	PI/KB (ALWAYS READ THEM BEFORE COMPLETING A TASK) STL 7 — 7.1 7.2 KB	STL 8 — 8.1 8.2 KB	IDEAS FOR RESOURCES
	Think about the words you use. Are they the vocabulary of ICT as a subject? Are there times when students achieve in ICT while learning another subject? Using a digital camera in history, perhaps. How is this recorded?			done with ICT when working in another subject.
Make a list of the ways in which you keep up to date with changes in technology.	This will be through a lot of routes. • Training courses • Exhibitions • Newspapers and magazines • The internet • Discussions with colleagues, pupils, your family • Television	26		30 There are many ways you do this, some of which you will not even realise. Think about what you know now compared to a year ago. How has it changed? Why?
Create a flow diagram to show what you do when equipment is faulty, and the school procedures for putting it right.	This will vary between schools. In some places you might just talk to the ICT coordinator, others may have a fault logging system on the computer network. Include things such as making the machine safe, marking it as faulty and checking the fault has been rectified.	6, 5, 5 8, 6, 9 8		11 27 This need not be complicated. Using call-outs in MS Word or PowerPoint will be sufficient, although you may prefer to use something more specialist such as mind-mapping software.

ACTIVITY	CONTENT COVERED	PI/KB (ALWAYS READ THEM BEFORE COMPLETING A TASK)		IDEAS FOR RESOURCES
		STL 7	STL 8	
		7.1 7.2 KB	8.1 8.2 KB	
				Ask your ICT coordinator, technician or someone else involved in the process to sign the diagram to show that it is accurate.
Ask a teacher(s) you work with to write a Witness Statement about your work in the classroom.	The Witness Statement needs to give examples to back up each point. It is not sufficient for the witness to say you are very good at your job, they must make sure it is clear how you meet the criteria for the NVQ.	1, 1, 6, 2, 2, 13, 3, 3, 19, 4, 4, 20, 5, 6, 21, 6, 7, 22 7, 8, 8, 9 9	1, 15, 2, 23 4, 6, 8, 9, 10, 12	You might need more than one Witness Statement to cover all the criteria. Some are to do with preparing resources, such as setting them up, others are to do with your teaching, and how you contribute to helping children learn.

Appendix 3:
Useful websites

Information about the NVQ

Training and Development Agency for Schools information on the National Occupational Standards:

■ www.tda.gov.uk/support-staff/developing-progressing/nos/supporting-teaching-and-learning-in-schools.aspx

Information and resources from Edexcel, one of the examining bodies for the NVQ:

■ www.edexcel.com/quals/nvq/teachasst/Pages/default.aspx

Online resources for working with children

For music making:

■ www.jamstudio.com
■ www.looplabs.com

For editing photos online:

■ www.pixlr.com/
■ www.picnik.com/
■ www.editor.pho.to/

For making 30 second movies from still photos:

■ http://animoto.com/

For drawing pictures online:

- www.queeky.com
- http://artpad.art.com/artpad/painter/
- www.billybear4kids.com/Learn2Draw/PaintProgram/drawing.htm

For translating your name into hieroglyphics:

- www.quizland.com/hiero.htm

To make your own speaking avatar:

- www.voki.com

Index